Merson

Richmond Crinkley, 1969

The Days Between

"it's futile, Merson"

...erson, 196...

...ver thought

...

Ministry

Books by Robert Anderson

Tea and Sympathy
All Summer Long
Silent Night, Lonely Night
The Days Between

THE

DAYS
BETWEEN

ROBERT ANDERSON

Random House : New York

FIRST PRINTING

Library of Congress Catalog Card Number: 65–20262

MANUFACTURED IN THE UNITED STATES OF AMERICA
By The Book Press, Brattleboro, Vt.

For *Teresa*

Cast of Characters

BARBARA IVES

MRS. WALKER

DAVID IVES

ROGER IVES

GEORGE HAWKINS

TED SEARS

Act One

Scene One

There are no sets—just levels, lights and props. Generally, stage right represents the house, with the family-kitchen room on the ground floor, and various bedrooms on slightly raised levels. The center area is a garden, where we may imagine a large tree; and the stage-left area is slightly raised to indicate a room over a converted barn.

The place is a New England college town, in the summer of the present. It is late afternoon.

As the curtain rises, BARBARA IVES *is in the kitchen, at the telephone. She is a lovely woman, in her late thirties, but there are lines of strain and tension in her face. Her smile is ready and almost pleading for kindness. On the top level of the house,* DAVID IVES, *her husband, sits before a typewriter, his eyes closed in troubled thought. Tied to a standing gooseneck lamp is a length of bright red silk. On a lower level,* ROGER, *the ten-year-old son—a manly youngster—is seated on the floor of his room, working on a collage. Barbara's mother,* MRS. WALKER, *is sitting at a table in the kitchen, staring at her daughter's back, trying by the force of the stare to make her turn around.* BARBARA *is quite aware of this, and tries to ignore it. Finally her call goes through.*

BARBARA (*On the phone*)   Mario ... Mrs. Ives ... I wanted to order something I'll pick up a little later . . . Is there any lobster in today . . . How much does it run? . . . Oh.

It sounds very high. Is that what it's been right along . . .
I guess I haven't ordered lobster in a long time. (*She becomes acutely aware of her mother's efforts to make her
turn around, and she turns the other way*) Well, I've got
to have them . . . I'm making a lobster salad . . . for oh . . .
two, maybe three. What would that come to? . . . I see . . .
well, then, I'll want some tomatoes. Three nice ones, and
some Boston lettuce, if you have it . . . French bread. Is
it fresh? . . . A pound of butter and . . . I may think of
what I want for dessert when I come by . . . Oh, you can
start getting it together now . . . Thank you.
  (*She hangs up; she continues to avoid her mother's
  look. She picks up a bud vase with a single rose in it,
  and starts to leave the kitchen for the garden*)

MRS. WALKER (*Has never taken her eyes from* BARBARA)
Barbara!

BARBARA (*Stops, but doesn't look around. When her mother
says nothing:*) Yes, Mother? (*Her mother just stares at
her back*) Mother, I don't want to talk about it any more.
Mr. Sears is coming, and that's that.
  (*She starts out again*)

MRS. WALKER Why?

BARBARA Because I want him to. It may seem a very small
and unimportant reason. But it is my reason.

MRS. WALKER What are Roger and I supposed to say to
David if he comes down and you're in the village?

BARBARA   Nothing.

MRS. WALKER   Then I'm going to my room, because I'm not going to lie to him.

BARBARA   I am not asking you to lie to him. Just say nothing. I want to tell him myself.

MRS. WALKER   If you will take my advice, when this man calls again . . . I believe you said he would call again from the road . . .

BARBARA   Mother!

MRS. WALKER   I just don't understand.

BARBARA (*Turns at last*)   What is so difficult to understand? A friend is coming to our village for one day . . . He calls and asks if he can take David and me to dinner, and I tell him David is working night and day on his book, and why doesn't he come *here* for dinner.

MRS. WALKER   *And* stay over the barn.

BARBARA (*Defensively*)   Yes.

MRS. WALKER   When you knew that it might upset David.

5

BARBARA   David has not come down for dinner for two weeks. He ...
(*But she does not go on. She leaves the house and goes to the barn, climbs the few steps to the room, puts the bud vase with the flower on a small table, and then sits on the bed. She stares out at nothing, and then closes her eyes tight. She doesn't want to think.* ROGER *begins to play his recorder in his room* ... DAVID *in his attic study reacts to this with a small frown, but he goes back to his thinking.* MRS. WALKER *notices the music, and comes across the garden and up the stairs.* BARBARA, *as she sees her mother entering:*) Mother, please.

MRS. WALKER   Should Roger be playing while his father's working?

BARBARA   No, but ...
(*She shrugs ... she cannot keep the boy quiet all day*)

MRS. WALKER (*Looks at* BARBARA *for a few moments—then goes on*)   Do you know what this book he is writing ... do you know what it means to him? (BARBARA *looks at her with impatience*) I've lived a lot longer than you have, Barbara ... and I'll tell you what I think. (*She is very grave about this*) I think, if he doesn't get this book written, he will die. All the years of teaching, this has always been—

BARBARA (*Interrupting*) Mother, my God. Where do you think I've been?

MRS. WALKER I'm saying to you, I think he would die.

BARBARA (*After a long pause, sadly*) And I'm telling you ... he's dead already.

MRS. WALKER Barbara!

BARBARA To this life, to this "contemptible" ... "grubby" life. Or as he says ... "cruddy."

MRS. WALKER But this summer ...

BARBARA But this summer. I have dreaded this summer. I have wanted to die rather than face this summer.

MRS. WALKER I don't understand.

BARBARA Because this book will never be written. And then?

MRS. WALKER I can't agree with you that it will never be written. Why, he's come bounding down the stairs some days ...

BARBARA Yes. Ready to fly. Ready to get drunk and celebrate. Suddenly in his mind, the book is written, the reviews are in, and everything will be different, and it's time to celebrate and make love . . . Only the love is sometimes so close to hate . . . I think he will kill me.

MRS. WALKER (*Sympathetically*) My baby.

BARBARA (*Shunning her*) No, Mother. Please.

MRS. WALKER (*After a moment*) Hold on. Believe me. Hold on . . . Don't do anything . . . anything . . . (*She doesn't say "foolish"*) And encourage him . . . There's always another summer.

BARBARA No . . . This summer. That's all there is . . . Somehow I know that. And I'm terrified.
(*In the house,* DAVID *finally calls from his study . . . a little harshly*)

DAVID Roge!
(ROGER *stops playing abruptly, upset and frowning. During the following,* MRS. WALKER *leaves the barn and moves back into the kitchen.* DAVID *realizes that he may have sounded too harsh; he comes down and stands in* ROGER's *door*)

ROGER I'm sorry.
(DAVID *is a young forty, intense, mercurial, moody, and sometimes charming*)

DAVID No. It's all right. You gotta play sometime . . . It's just that I was getting something working up there.

ROGER (*Flatly*) Oh . . . Good.

DAVID (*Seeing the collage on the floor*) What're you making?

ROGER Oh, a thing.

DAVID What kind of thing?

ROGER It's a . . . oh, something. It was supposed to be a surprise for Mom . . . for her anniversary. I mean, you know, your anniversary, day after tomorrow.

DAVID You do this kind of thing well.

ROGER (*Shrugging it off*) Oh.

DAVID (*Looks at him a long moment, then*) Look, Roge, when this book is written—and it started coming better today—when it's written, and it . . . dazzles the world (*He smiles*) let's you and me get us a couple of fishing rods and a rowboat and we'll go out in the middle of the Lake, and we'll just sit and get to know each other. Okay?

ROGER (*Embarrassed, looks at the floor*) Yeah . . . sure.

DAVID (*The lack of enthusiasm registers . . . but he smiles*) Okay.
(*He looks at his son for a few moments, then he turns*

9

and goes up to his attic room ... rips a paper out of
his typewriter ... and puts another one in ... and
starts typing. A young man of twenty-six comes into
the garden, looking at the house—tentatively. He
carries a book)

BARBARA (*Has been coming down the steps from the barn*)
Yes?

GEORGE   Mrs. Ives?

BARBARA   Yes?

GEORGE   You won't remember me, but I was a student here
in your husband's advanced writing course ... six or seven
years ago. I'm George Hawkins.

BARBARA (*Holding out her hand*)   Oh, I'm sorry. I should
have remembered. How are you?

GEORGE (*Rather shy*)   Fine, thanks.
(MRS. WALKER *has gone inside the house. She goes*
up to her room, and sits)

BARBARA (*The master's wife*)   David was very proud of
you ... the book, and the prize.

GEORGE (*Pleased*)   Oh ... I didn't hear from him, and I ...

BARBARA   Well, you know. The absent-minded professor ...
You're speaking at the writers' conference, aren't you?

GEORGE   Kind of ridiculous, but I am. There's nothing I can
say that Mr. Ives can't say better. But ...
   (*He shrugs*)

BARBARA   Oh, students always like to get a glimpse of someone who's just made it ... a certain glamor.
   (*She flatters him nicely*)

GEORGE   I ... uh ... I've got a new book out today, as a
matter of fact. And I thought I'd ... I want to bring a copy
to Mr. Ives. (*He holds out the book*)

BARBARA   Oh, that's very kind of you.

GEORGE   Yes, well ... It's—it's dedicated to him.

BARBARA   (GEORGE *doesn't notice a slight frown pass over her
face*) How nice.

GEORGE   I should have dedicated my first book to him, but
that had to be for my mother and father.

BARBARA   Naturally.

GEORGE   But this one is his. I guess all my work will be his
in a sense.

BARBARA (*Protesting nicely*) Oh...

GEORGE No, that's true. For so many of us. Is he in?

BARBARA He's upstairs working.

GEORGE They told me he wasn't teaching the summer term.

BARBARA He isn't. He's writing his book.

GEORGE (*Very pleased*) Oh, God, that's wonderful. (*He impulsively shakes* BARBARA'*s hand*) Excuse me, but I can't tell you how happy I am that he's got down to it—finally got—down to it.

BARBARA Yes, he has.

GEORGE God, I wish him luck.

BARBARA Thank you.

GEORGE I remember how impatient he was, never being able to get down to another book, all these years . . . with all our stories and stuff piling up on his desk. Did his other ex-students keep sending him reams of manuscripts the way I did?

BARBARA Yes.

GEORGE Why didn't he tell us to go to hell? Excuse me, but...

BARBARA Well, he's telling everyone to go to hell this summer.

GEORGE That's great. His first book was ... well, I can only say I studied it backwards and forwards, and even typed out pages from it, hoping to pick up something of what he had . . . in it. It's wonderful he's down to it at last. (*An uneasy look passes between them*) He'll make us all look silly.

BARBARA Oh...

GEORGE Oh, he will, with his standards. I ... I found them murderous when I finally got down to writing . . . I couldn't ... well, I mean I tried, and I always kept them in mind ... somewhere way back here ... but finally, I just had to, well, write and let someone else worry about the masterpieces... He'll do that.

BARBARA I enjoyed your book a lot.

GEORGE Oh, thanks. Do you think you and Mr. Ives could come to the Inn tonight and have dinner with me? Help me celebrate this?
      (*He holds up the book*)

13

BARBARA I'm afraid we couldn't. We . . . well, we can't. Maybe sometime during the conference, though.

GEORGE Oh.

BARBARA As a matter of fact, I was on my way into the village to pick up some things I've ordered. Can I give you a lift?

GEORGE It's only a few steps, and I'd like to give this to Mr. Ives personally, if I could.

BARBARA He sometimes goes on and on . . . you know how it is. Midnight, or—

GEORGE If you wouldn't mind, I won't be in the way. I'll sit in the garden, just on the chance.

BARBARA You won't be in the way, but—

GEORGE I don't mind waiting. It's . . . oh, I know it's nothing new for him to have ex-students dedicate books to him . . . but it's new for me.

BARBARA (*Charmed by his young enthusiasm, but worried too*) I understand.

GEORGE What have there been, dedications . . . a dozen or more?

BARBARA (*The number is a little painful, but she smiles*) Yes.

GEORGE That must be something of a record.

BARBARA I imagine it is.

GEORGE I remember his dedication to you in his book . . . probably because I could never understand it.

BARBARA It was a private joke.

GEORGE "For Barbara and her violet eyes." Are they violet?

BARBARA No. (GEORGE *is puzzled*) When we met, when he'd come back from the war, he had a favorite quotation . . . I can't remember it exactly, but it was something about . . . if you have only two loaves of bread left to your name, sell one and with the money buy violets to feed the soul.

GEORGE That's lovely. (*Then suddenly*) I'm going to be married next month.

BARBARA Congratulations.

GEORGE I hope it won't embarrass you when I say I used to hope my wife would be like you. She is a little.

BARBARA I am embarrassed.

GEORGE I'd like her to meet you, but she didn't come up with me.

BARBARA I'm sorry.

GEORGE Mr. Ives used to say that any of his students who were thinking of getting married right off should have their girls check with you and find out what a hell it is being married to a struggling writer.

BARBARA Well...

GEORGE I was going to get married back then, when I was leaving here . . . but your husband scared me off, and I'm glad he did . . . There were some rugged times, and I don't think I could have put a girl through them . . . (*Smiles broadly*) Anyway, I don't think I really loved her.

BARBARA I've got to leave you. (*Shakes hands with him*) Congratulations again. It sounds wonderful . . . If you're gone when I come back, I hope we see you sometime during the conference.

GEORGE Thank you.

BARBARA (*Quietly, after a moment*) Being a writer yourself, you'll understand any mood he's in . . . any . . . well, you'll understand.

GEORGE Of course.

16

BARBARA (*On the way out*) There's iced tea in the refrig if you get thirsty.

> (*And she is gone.* GEORGE *sits on a bench in the garden and ruffles the pages of his book, looks at the dust-jacket blurbs*)

DAVID (*Up in the attic, he has heard* BARBARA *leave. He rises with the paper he has been writing on in one hand and listens. At the moment he is keyed up, almost like a boy with a project under way*) Roge.

ROGER (*Coming to his bedroom door, hesitant*) Yes?

DAVID Was that your mother who went out?

ROGER Yes.

DAVID (*Comes down the stairs, bringing his son along as he passes him, arm around his shoulders*) I want you to do something for me . . . I want you to go out in the garden and cut some flowers . . . oh, about so high, and bring them in. No questions.

ROGER What kind of flowers?

DAVID Any violets out there this time of year?

ROGER Maybe a few.

DAVID Well, get them and anything else . . . I want to get this set up before she comes back.
   (*He folds the paper he has been carrying*)

ROGER There's someone outside.

DAVID (*Turns, a look of annoyance*) What?
   (*He goes to the door and looks out at* GEORGE, *who is now standing*)

GEORGE George Hawkins, sir.

DAVID (*Friendly*) Sure, I know. (*He comes out*) Good to see you . . . You met my son, Roger?

GEORGE Hello.

ROGER Hello.

DAVID Roger's president of the local kids' garden club. He's going to cut some flowers for me. (*To* ROGER) Let's go, man. We don't have much time. . .
   (*He playfully shoves* ROGER *along.* ROGER *disappears towards the back*)

GEORGE I won't keep you.

DAVID It's all right. It's good to see you. Congratulations on the prize. I'm sorry as hell I didn't get a note off . . . but

I worked my tail off all spring, all year for that matter, trying to clear the decks to write this summer.

GEORGE   Mrs. Ives told me you were writing. I think that's great.

DAVID   Yeah, it is just that . . . great. God, I've been stalled for so long, waiting for just the right thing, you know. Hell, I was beginning to believe that old saw . . . "Those who can, do. Those who can't, teach." You working on something new? (GEORGE *shyly but proudly presents his book*) Good God, not another one out already?

GEORGE   It was written before the other one. But they wouldn't publish it until . . . well . . .

DAVID   Till you were a success. I know. (*The schoolmaster*) You're not pawning off second-rate goods on the basis of your first success, are you?

GEORGE   Actually, this one's better . . . I think.

DAVID   Good. All the crap being written. Don't want my boys writing crud.

GEORGE   (*Anxious for him to see the dedication, but not wanting to point to it*) I hope it isn't, sir.

DAVID   (*Trying to be offhand about it*)   Look, your name's George, my name's David. (*Goes right on*) Two books out in one year . . . and I've waited how many lousy years to get a second one out?

(He opens the book and sees the dedication, which he had almost suspected and feared)

GEORGE   I suppose I should have asked your permission to dedicate it to you.

DAVID *(After a moment)*   Thanks, George. I hope your book isn't that flowery.

DAVID *(Very sincerely)*   I happen to think it's true . . . You *are* one of the great teachers.

DAVID   Look, I told you in class—I've told every class— that if any of you became famous, I wouldn't go around claiming you.

GEORGE   I guess we just claimed you.

DAVID   Yeah.

GEORGE   Mrs. Ives says this makes over a dozen.

DAVID *(Smiles)*   You'd think people would have someone else to dedicate their books to . . . mothers, fathers, wives . . .

GEORGE   My next one will be to my wife. I'm getting married in a month.

DAVID   Well...!

GEORGE   Remember the talk we had six years ago, when I left here?

DAVID   Forgive me, but I don't. What did I shoot my mouth off about?

GEORGE   I was going to get married, right out of school.

DAVID   And what did I say?

GEORGE   You persuaded me against it . . . and you were right. You said getting started was hell, and no man had a right to put a woman through that hell.

DAVID   Well, it was hell, wasn't it?

GEORGE   Yes.

DAVID   A guy alone is willing to starve and live in a garret . . . eat junk, even go hungry . . . But if you have a wife, and any sense of decency, it kills you to see her starve. (*With vehemence*) You can't watch her starve. And so you compromise . . . and pretty soon you've compromised yourself right out of your talent. You can get it back, but it's a hell of a lot of work . . . (*He is a little embarrassed at being carried away . . . he looks at the book in his hand*) You like them at Random House?

GEORGE   Yes, very much.

DAVID   Maybe I'll send them mine when I'm done.

GEORGE   I guess any publisher would want your book.

DAVID   Oh . . .

GEORGE   (*Eager to do something for his master*)   But if you *do* send it to Random House, why . . . uh.

DAVID   You'll put in a good word for me. (*They both smile*) I suppose you're up to your ears in literary teas. Everybody wants your opinion on everything.

GEORGE   It's a little hectic . . . and ridiculous.

DAVID   Where you living?

GEORGE   In New York. We're going on a honeymoon to Jamaica . . . and then we've got a nice little apartment, small, but a duplex kind of, with fireplaces, on East Tenth Street.

DAVID   We might want something like that. If you hear of anything.

GEORGE   You wouldn't leave here, would you? (DAVID *looks at him*) When I was here in college, I always

wanted to be a writer so's I could have a life like you have here ... Everything's so ...
(*He can't describe it, it's so pleasant*)

DAVID (*Looks at him a long moment, then quietly*)   George, you're a big boy now ... This is no place ... This is Nothing ... This is Death.

GEORGE (*Is embarrassed. He doesn't know what to say*)   I ... I wanted you and your wife to come to dinner with me tonight at the Inn. But she says you have other plans.

DAVID   I don't know what her plans are ... Maybe she just was trying to protect me. I bite her head off when she lets anyone bust up my working schedule ... But I have plans. This is our anniversary.

GEORGE   Oh, congratulations.

DAVID   *And,* besides, I think I licked the ABC's of that book up there today ... You know how that is.

GEORGE   That's great.

DAVID   So I want to celebrate. I owe her diamond bracelets and orchids and Jamaica ... but that'll come later. All I'm managing tonight is a humble letter of apology for the misery, and a bunch of home-grown flowers ... (ROGER *has come back in, with a handful of flowers*) Any violets, Roge?

ROGER   They're all gone.

DAVID   Oh, hell!

GEORGE   I'll go along, then . . . But it would be nice to see you sometime during the conference.

DAVID   George, I'm not going to be over . . . You remember what I used to say. Every writer should put a big sign on his desk: N—O—W. Well, N—O—W is now, George. And frankly it's N—O—W or N—E—V—E—R.

GEORGE (*Disagreeing*)   Oh.

DAVID (*Firmly*)   Yes! You're what—twenty-six? I'm forty. And that's a desperate age.

GEORGE (*After a moment*)   I . . . uh . . . see some of the fellows around in New York . . . Peter Wesley, Harry Barrett—

DAVID   Tell them to save up five bucks for teacher's book.

GEORGE   And I'll tell Random House to hold the presses.

DAVID   Yeah, do that.

GEORGE   Goodbye, Roger.
        (ROGER *has gone with the flowers towards the table inside*)

ROGER   Goodbye.

DAVID   Thanks for the book . . . and the purple prose.

GEORGE   I'm sorry if it embarrasses you.

DAVID   As they say . . . "that's my problem." My best to your
bride, and tell her "Courage," but then you're a nice guy
and not a son-of-a-bitch like me. (*Turns to* ROGER) You
didn't hear that, see. (*He turns and waves again to
George. He looks at the book for a moment, reads the in-
scription, snaps the book shut and enters the house*) Oh,
I should have told you, Roge. I don't want to use that
bowl. I'm sorry, but I want to use this.
(*He gets out a lower vase*)

ROGER   They won't look so hot in this.

DAVID   Can't you just cut them off shorter?

ROGER   Yeah, but . . .
(*He holds a long-stemmed flower next to the low
bowl*)

DAVID   Do the best you can. The bowl is important . . . First
flowers I ever sent your mother came in that . . . God, I
hate having just this junk out of the garden.

ROGER   She likes these.

DAVID You're sure no violets?

ROGER Yes.

DAVID I planted a whole flock of violets out back of the barn years ago.

ROGER It's just too late for them . . . Is this for something special?

DAVID Yeah. Our anniversary, for one thing.

ROGER But that's three days off yet.

DAVID I've decided it's going to be tonight. By the authority vested in me as head of this household . . . Is that okay with you?

ROGER (*Worried*) Sure.

DAVID What's the matter?

ROGER Nothing.

DAVID And I want to put this letter to her leaning against it somewhere . . . (*He tries out a couple of places*) And then we're going to scram until she's read it.

ROGER (*Still arranging flowers*) What's in the letter?

26

DAVID   What you would call gooey-mushy love . . . Yeah, well, that's what's in it . . . And look, Roger, I want you to make yourself scarce. Take you and your grandmother to the village for a feed. Gorge yourself on hot dogs, and go to the movies, and stay and see it twice.
(*He gets out his wallet, but he finds he has only one bill—a five-dollar bill. He hesitates*)

ROGER   I've got some allowance saved. You can give it to me later.

DAVID (*Hating to be short of money*)   No. Here, dammit.

ROGER (*Not wanting to take anything from his father*)   I can manage it.

DAVID   No. Here! (ROGER *makes no move to take it, his hands busy with the flowers.* DAVID *flares momentarily*) Here! (*He stuffs the bill in* ROGER's *shirt pocket. He moves away a moment, angry, then in an attempt to calm down, he goes on*) That's nice.

ROGER   The bowl's still not right.

DAVID   It'll be all right. When's your next flower show? I can come see you do something real fancy.

ROGER   They're all over.

DAVID   Summer . . . flowers are just getting going.

ROGER   Most of the flowers are in the spring.

DAVID   I used to know all about flowers . . . Oh, I couldn't arrange them, or grow them like you . . . but when your mother and I were courting, there was a flower shop on the corner where she lived . . . and I'd always bring something. Maybe just one flower, but always something with style. Remember style, Roge . . . A man's life gets up to here with crud. We weren't sent on this earth just to pay bills, count our change and live in crud. (*He smiles, embarrassed that he's been carried away. He gets out a bottle of whiskey during the next, and pours himself a good drink, and goes on*) I remember one time, I brought her just one white violet. Crazy . . . me walking up the street with this one white violet wrapped in wax paper. But whatever it was, whatever flower, it had to be perfect . . . because your mother was perfect. (*Again he has become vehement on the subject. He smiles to relieve the embarrassment*) Thanks for going to the movies for me . . . for clearing the decks. I'll do as much for you some day when you want to neck with your girl. (BARBARA *appears in the garden, her arms filled with packages and grocery bags.* DAVID, *herding* ROGER *up the stairs*) Okay, let's clear out.

ROGER   I've got to help her with the packages.

DAVID   She'll manage. I want her to read the letter.

ROGER (*Desperate*)   But I've got to.

28

DAVID (*Sharp*) Roger! Now come on. (ROGER *turns and darts into his room and sits on his bed, his head down, shoulders hunched, and hands pressed between his knees.* DAVID *moves up the stairs and waits.* BARBARA *comes in. She sees the arrangement and the letter, and the bottle of whiskey. She puts down her packages, goes to the letter, which is leaning against the flowers. Hesitantly she starts to read the letter. She knows what will be in it. There have been others like it, but she is nevertheless touched. She is also desperate, and in her total confusion of feelings, she turns away and starts to cry. When* DAVID *hears her crying, he is disturbed, and comes down the stairs and over to her, and hugs her head to him*) Oh, honey, don't. God, I wanted to say it all to you, but I'm a lousy talker, you know . . . and I wanted to get it all out before you said anything . . . just everything. What a bastard I've been. How sorry I am . . . I know I've said it before, but it's going to be different now, Barbara. I don't know how you've stood it. (*He crouches beside her*) God, Barbara, I want to fly. Fly with me, Barbara. Oh, don't say anything. Whatever you're going to say, please forget it. Please . . . I know it's wrong to just rush at you like this and ask you to forget everything. But I am. I've got it licked, and it's going to be different. It's got to be different. (BARBARA's *tears subside a bit, but she is still crying*) Jesus, I can't stand to see you cry. I know how it's been. But that's over. When the book is done, we'll burn down this house and every piece of meanness that's in it . . . No more lousy teaching. No more betrayal. Only love, endless love like it used to be . . . (*Her sobs have died down . . . But he is now baffled, a little put off that his confession and plea*

29

for love are not finding a different response) What's the matter?

BARBARA Nothing . . . I . . . (DAVID *moves away, puzzled, and looks at her*) I don't know. (*She looks down and tries to hold back the tears again, then*) It's all right . . . we'll . . . we'll celebrate.

DAVID Barbara?

BARBARA Oh, I don't know . . . I always seem to end up the bitch.

DAVID (*Coming to comfort her*) No . . . How?

BARBARA This morning—while you were working—Ted Sears called.

DAVID You?

BARBARA He's changed his mind and decided to come to the writers' conference.

DAVID So?

BARBARA When I was in New York last fall they were so damned nice to me, I said if he ever came back to the college for a visit, he must stay with us over the barn.

DAVID Oh.

BARBARA He called and said he'd like to take us to dinner. I told him I never knew when you were going to be free, so why didn't he come here for dinner . . . and then . . . I just asked him to stay over the barn for the one night. But he's calling back from the road. I said I'd have to check with you—and I'll tell him he can't come. (*But this thought obviously upsets her, and* DAVID *notes this. He turns away, upset*) I couldn't disturb you at your work. You would have killed me if I'd interrupted your work.

DAVID (*Flaring*) Sure, I go around killing people.

BARBARA I didn't say—

DAVID (*Taking off*) I know I'm an impossible bastard. Only everybody seems to forget why.

BARBARA We know why, David.

DAVID Then how could you invite this crap artist to stay with us?

BARBARA I told him I'd have to check with you . . . I'll tell him he can't come.

DAVID God, you know how important this summer is to me . . . to *us,* I thought. You know I slaved all year, extra classes, tutoring, reviewing crappy books like Mr. Ted Sears writes, till I was blind from reading . . . just to buy this summer . . . a summer I wouldn't have to teach . . . a summer when I could at last get down to this God damned book.

BARBARA Do you hate this book so? You always call it "this God damned book."

DAVID Because I always have to put it off . . . and it keeps nagging at me. And I dabble with it over a weekend, and I just get a little excited about it . . . and classes start. And now I've just got it licked, and the great man arrives. The great husband!

BARBARA He doesn't have to interfere with your work.

DAVID What am I supposed to do—ignore him? Or sit around and discuss the sentimental trash he writes?

BARBARA It's not trash.

DAVID Successful, sentimental trash.

BARBARA The college wouldn't have him up here if it were trash.

DAVID (*Don't be so sure*) Oh . . . ?

32

BARBARA You've just come to hate everything that's successful.

DAVID (*Stung*) That's not true. I just hate mediocrity . . . in all its forms: in writing, in living, in— And he is mediocre. Christ, there *are* standards.

BARBARA (*Flat, despairing*) He said he'd call back, from somewhere on the road. I'll tell him he can't stay here. We can't eat with him . . . Oh, God, I don't know what to do.

DAVID (*After a long moment, obviously a very serious note*) Neither do I. (BARBARA *looks up at the new tone*) Shall I give up? Shall I give up the whole God damned mess? Do you want me to be a teacher all my life? Did you marry a teacher?

BARBARA I married you.

DAVID Oh, that's an evasion. What me? Back in the sand dunes, fifteen years ago, we didn't lie on the beach and dream glorious dreams of my teaching English Composition all my life, did we?

BARBARA No, we didn't, but—

DAVID Would you have married me if I'd said I'm going to be a teacher?

33

BARBARA   I married you, not what you were going to become.

DAVID   Damn it, Barbara, that's a lie. I was a bright and shining hero just back from the war, and I was going to be a bright and shining success . . . and that's how we talked, and loved. Do you think I could have loved you that way if I'd felt that this was all I was going to be? . . . It was the promise that I wouldn't be like all the other cruddy people that gave me— (*He can't express strength, virility, power*) that made us talk that way.

BARBARA   All kids do that.

DAVID   You mean we're not kids . . . Settle . . . Settle for this . . .
        (*He waves his arm in derision*)

BARBARA   David, stop it! Why?

DAVID   (*The letter he wrote her is on the table by him. He rips it in two during this speech*)   Because I'm mad . . . mad and disappointed. When you knew how important this was to me . . . me at least . . . Because I want to tell you now . . . that if I ever stop believing in this . . . this kid's dream, that this book or some book will change our lives . . . then watch out! This isn't living. This is failure, betrayal, compromise and death! What the hell is he that he should come and live with us? I've never even met him.

BARBARA   I'll tell him he can't come.

DAVID   I know how nice he was to you in New York, and I know how starry-eyed you got over their perfect marriage, but my God, what's all this . . . (*He starts poking in the shopping bags*) Wine.

BARBARA   David, stop it!

DAVID   And lobster. When is the last time we had lobster?

BARBARA   Stop it! *This* happens to be . . . not the day after tomorrow . . . *this* day is his anniversary. If Meg had lived, this would have been their eighteenth anniversary. I wanted to try. I thought he'd be lonely.

DAVID   *He*'d be lonely!

BARBARA   Oh, David, I won't have him come.

DAVID   Wine for his loneliness. Five, six dollars a bottle.

BARBARA   A dollar sixty-nine.

DAVID   But still money . . . Barbara, how did you think I got through last year . . . all those books reviewed, all that tutoring . . . no lunches . . . I got through it because I kept a list . . . and each time, I wrote in . . . five dollars, ten dollars . . . that'll buy a day, a half day . . . Do you think I like nagging about money all the time? I want to be like Ted. I want to be able to take you to the restaurants he took you to . . . buy the clothes you saw him buy for his wife. When you came back and talked about those things, you should have seen your eyes.

BARBARA I wasn't saying I wanted those things. You take everything as a criticism. I can't praise anything or anyone without your feeling I'm running you down.

DAVID You are . . . Do you think I like my son hating me?

BARBARA He doesn't.

DAVID He does. Because I'm stingy. Don't you think I want to be able to throw money around too? Here, take a thousand and buy a dress. But it can't be that way as long as I'm here grubbing. And every dollar or dollar sixty-nine spent on wine, means that much longer I have to grub to buy free time to do the work that's going to get us out of this . . . I loathe myself right now, talking like this . . . but what can I do? . . . It sounds ridiculous to you, but when I go to a stationery store to buy paper for this book, I buy the cheapest paper I can find, and then you . . . (*The phone rings.* DAVID *is right at it. He picks it up*) Hello.

BARBARA (*Wants to take the phone*) David.

DAVID Oh, yes, hello . . . Yes, I know she did . . .

36

BARBARA (*Whispering*) Please.

DAVID No, it's going to be quite all right . . . No. No . . .
Come along. She's got everything ready . . . Any time you
arrive . . . Yes. Goodbye.

BARBARA Oh, David.

DAVID You wanted to see him . . . My God, you haven't
seen anyone in weeks . . . see him. You're all set for him,
aren't you—lobster, wine . . . (*He ticks them off on his
way out, and then comes across a wrapped bouquet of
flowers*) And what's this? Flowers.

BARBARA He ordered them. The florist saw me passing
and—

DAVID Hell, then, we don't need these.
(*He picks up his own bowl of flowers*)

BARBARA (*Rushing to stop him*) David.
(DAVID *slams the bowl of flowers into the corner.*
BARBARA *turns away, almost as though hit herself.*
ROGER, *when the voices have been raised after the
phone call, has started downstairs, and now he comes
into the kitchen, and looks at his father with a men-
acing look*)

DAVID (*Sees his son standing there. He is still angry, but
ashamed and appalled at what he has done, and at the*

*general hopelessness of it. He bows his head and rushes
out the door)* Oh, Christ!
    (It is a half-sob . . . and he is gone)

BARBARA *(Follows him)* David!
    (She stands in the door, upset, wanting to be alone)

ROGER *(Inside the house)* I hope he doesn't come back. I
hope he never—

BARBARA *(Turns angrily on him, and grabs his arm)* Don't
you say that. Don't you ever let me hear you say that
again.

ROGER *(Pulling away from her and running up to his room)*
I can't help it. I hate him. I hate him!

BARBARA *(The last thing she wants to do is talk to* ROGER,
but it must be done. She follows him up) Roger.

MRS. WALKER *(Comes out to the hall)* Barbara.

BARBARA Just a minute, Mother. (MRS. WALKER *lingers)*
Please. (MRS. WALKER *goes back into her room)* Roger.
(She goes into ROGER'S *room)* Do you understand? I don't
want you ever to say that about your father. Now what
goes on between your father and me is . . . between us.

ROGER He makes you cry.

BARBARA   Well, I make him cry too.

ROGER   I never saw him cry.

BARBARA   Still he cries . . . and you make him cry.

ROGER   How can I make him cry? I never say anything to him.

BARBARA   Yes. Exactly.

ROGER   What is there to say?

BARBARA   I don't know. Maybe "thanks" once in a while.
(*She is sitting next to him on the bed*)

ROGER   For what?

BARBARA   (*Controls her anger, realizing how little he can understand*)   Didn't it ever occur to you that he'd perhaps rather be off somewhere on the farthest star? But he isn't. He's here. And until you know what it is not to have a father here, you don't know anything about it. He is here . . . if only for you to hate.

ROGER   I don't think you really mean any of this. You just think you have to say it to me because I'm a child.

BARBARA   That's not true.

ROGER   You can't love him.

BARBARA (*She starts to grab him, and then stops*)   Don't ever talk that way, Roger.

ROGER   How can you love him?

BARBARA   You have no business asking that question, but I'll tell you . . . Because it wasn't always this way . . . So I have memory—and hope. Oh, and more than that. You can't understand.

ROGER   What's going to be so different when he's written this book?

BARBARA   Something will be different for your father. He'll think of himself differently . . . and then he'll be more . . . more fun to live with.

ROGER   What if he never writes it?

BARBARA (*This has struck very deep, but she doesn't let on*) Don't say that.

ROGER   I went up there the other day.

BARBARA   You know you're not supposed to.

ROGER   But I did . . . and there was nothing.

40

BARBARA (*Closes her eyes*) Sometimes it takes months of just thinking . . . He said he got going on it today.

ROGER (*Shakes his head wisely: "You can believe that if you want to." He takes the five-dollar bill from his pocket*) Here.

BARBARA What's this?

ROGER He gave me this to take Grandma to supper and the movies tonight, so you could be alone.

BARBARA I want you to keep it. I want you to go.

ROGER I don't want his money.

BARBARA Roger! It's my money too. Now take it, and I want you to take your grandmother into the village, and eat, and see the movies, and try to . . . forget all this. (*She knows he can't, and smiles her knowing at him*) Eat a lot of hot dogs, with mustard, and relish—the works.

ROGER (*Without much conviction*) Okay.
(BARBARA *leaves* ROGER'*s room and is going to her own room, but her mother, who has been on the alert, calls*)

MRS. WALKER Barbara, I'd like to have a word with you.

41

BARBARA   Mother, I want to bathe and—

MRS. WALKER   Barbara, I must talk to you.
(*Obviously she has been waiting anxiously, searching her mind for what to say, and she has it lined up*)

BARBARA (*Entering her mother's room*)   I want you and
Roger to go to the village for supper and the movies, and
then I want you to take him to the cottage at the Lake for
tonight.

MRS. WALKER (*Ignoring this*)   Barbara, I know I am no
longer your mother, in a sense. Being dependent on you
robs me of a mother's authority. And I suppose that those
who have made a botch of their own lives have no right
to advise others.

BARBARA (*Moving to go*)   Not now, Mother.

MRS. WALKER   I made a botch of my life because I let my
husband, your father, walk out. I was stupid and full of
pride and full of ideas about what were my rights. But I
wanted to tell you . . . I don't know what ideas you got
during those long years we were alone together . . . I
probably said some terrible things about your father. But
no matter how terrible he was, if I had it to do over again,
I would have put up with anything, rather than have lived
the way we had to live when he left . . . and to end like
this, dependent on handouts from my daughter's husband. *Anything*.

BARBARA Mother...

MRS. WALKER I sit in those beauty parlors and I hear women say casually, "Oh, what I wouldn't give to be free." What do they think they're going to find? They're going to find loneliness, that's what they're going to find. And then they'll do anything to get away from loneliness, and they hope each man will marry them, only he doesn't. And then comes God only knows what . . . Oh, I didn't travel on that road. There was only Ralph, and Ralph—Well...
(She thinks something over)

BARBARA Mother, I don't want Roger to hear any more of those arguments. So I want you and him to go—

MRS. WALKER Do you have the faintest idea what it means at your age to be left alone in the world with no money and a child of ten?

BARBARA Mother, what are you talking about?

MRS. WALKER David walked out, didn't he? Like your father. Do you think it was anything bigger with your father? Do you think there was thunder and lightning that night? He just walked out and never came back. And you sit here getting ready to entertain a visitor.

BARBARA Mother...

MRS. WALKER I know what goes on in that room when he comes down drunk, but I don't care, and neither should you. And you'd better go out and find your husband if you don't want to end your days living in Roger's house mortified that you have to ask for a few dollars for a summer hat . . . What is so important about seeing this man?

BARBARA (*Flaring*) There is nothing important about seeing him. If we can't extend a little compassion, a little hospitality, to help a man over a difficult day.

MRS. WALKER Now, Barbara!

BARBARA His wife was dying, and still they could find time to be kind to me. If we can't . . . I don't want to talk about it.

MRS. WALKER If you have any sense, you will not see this man when he arrives. I will show him to his room—or Roger will—and I will tell him you are ill . . . or something.

BARBARA (*Firm*) I want to see him.

MRS. WALKER Why?

BARBARA I just want to see him . . . to talk to someone.

MRS. WALKER Talk to me.

44

BARBARA   I want you and Roger to go into the village, and then to the Lake. I do not want Roger here when David comes back. I cannot explain any more to Roger . . . and I don't want to argue any more with you.

MRS. WALKER   You don't know what you're doing.

BARBARA   Maybe I don't.

MRS. WALKER   I will tell you.

BARBARA   (*In anguish as she rushes out*)   I don't want to hear . . . I don't want to know.
(*She rushes down the stairs to the kitchen and leans against the table, breathing hard. Then she sinks down into the chair and stares at the table*)

The lights fade out

Scene Two

As the lights come up TED SEARS *is pulling on a shirt in the room over the barn. He is an attractive man of around forty, giving a sense of maturity in contrast to* DAVID's *almost boyish impulsiveness.* MRS. WALKER *is in the kitchen. After a moment,* ROGER *emerges from the kitchen carrying a small tray. On it are two glasses, a bowl of ice, some tonic water and a vodka bottle. Under his arm he is clutching a recorder. He stands under* TED's *window for a moment, trying to decide if it's all right to go up.* TED *sees him.*

TED   Hi.

ROGER   You had your nap?

TED   Yes.

ROGER   I've got some pain killer for you.

TED   What?
      (ROGER *shows him the tray*)

TED   Come on up.

ROGER (*Coming up the stairs*)   Have a good nap?

46

TED Yes. I was bushed from the drive. Your mother still resting?

ROGER No, she's in her room dressing, I guess. Something. She called out I was to bring you this.

TED I could have waited for the others.

ROGER Well, Mom's not drinking, and Dad's . . . not around.

TED You're the man of all work around here, aren't you?

ROGER It just happened that way today. I'm usually not much help. I think I forgot to tell you how to work the shower.

TED I figured it out . . . You having a drink?

ROGER Some tonic . . . keep you company. I like ice. I'm an ice-eater.

TED (*Pouring him a drink*) Are you?
       (*Hands him the drink*)

ROGER Uh . . . Mom said I couldn't keep this.
       (*He holds out the recorder*)

TED Oh?

47

ROGER   Yeah. She said to thank you very much, but I couldn't keep it. It's too good or something.
(BARBARA *comes from her bathroom into her bedroom. She is fully dressed and ready, but she just sits in a chair and stares at the window—thinking, puzzling, afraid to go down*)

TED   Oh, well ... I ... Well, that's too bad.

ROGER   It's complicated, but you see, my father bought me one ... It's not as good as this one ... and well, he bought it because he'd broken another one I had ... and ... I'm not supposed to play while he's working, and ... anyway ... I can't keep this. Thanks.
(*From time to time* ROGER *sucks ice into his mouth, and either talks around it ... or slips it back into the glass before he talks*)

TED   I'm sorry.

ROGER   Uh ... I tried that out. Do you think they'll take it back? I haven't got any diseases or anything.

TED (*Smiles*)   I'll do something with it.

ROGER   How did you know I played the recorder?

TED   When your mother was in New York, she looked for one for you.

48

ROGER   You shopped with her?

TED   Yes. She helped me to do some shopping for my wife
. . . who was sick at the time.

ROGER   Oh, yes. I'm sorry about . . . that.

TED   Thanks.

ROGER   Mom said she was a nice woman.

TED   She was.

ROGER   Mom talked a lot about you and your wife when
she got back.

TED   Did she?

ROGER   I never had anything die except a dog. I cried for
almost a week. That was when I was a kid.

TED   Sure.

ROGER   I don't think I'd cry now. But it was terrible.

TED   Yes, it is.
        (*He answers* ROGER *very simply, not making any-
        thing emotional about it*)

ROGER   I got over it.

TED   Sure.

ROGER   Mom wanted me to get another dog . . . but I didn't want one. He's buried out back . . . I'll show you sometime.

TED   I'd like to see it.

ROGER   I used to keep it kind of nice . . . It's just a stone now.

TED   Well . . .

ROGER   Mom says you're famous. (TED *shrugs*) We've got your books. I'm not allowed to read them, but we've got them.

TED   I'm flattered.

ROGER   Why can't I read them?

TED   I guess they're about things you wouldn't understand.

ROGER   Oh, sex.

TED   Among other things.

50

ROGER   Can I interview you? We've got to interview someone this summer if we want to write for the school paper.

TED   You want to be a writer?

ROGER   No. I can't even spell. Mom can't spell either. She
does all right on three-letter words, but after that . . . wow!
She has to write it all out in pencil, then she looks up most
of the words, and then she copies it in ink.

TED   (*Begins to be more and more conscious that* BARBARA *is
not appearing, and though he is enjoying this boy, he
wonders when* BARBARA *is coming*)   That's rugged.

ROGER   What sort of questions should I ask you?

TED   Oh . . .

ROGER   Do your kids like you?

TED   (*Taken aback a little by the question, smiles*)   I don't
have any kids.

ROGER   Oh.

TED   We wanted them. We just didn't have them.

ROGER   I'll bet if you had them, they'd like you.

TED   (*He is very touched by this*)   Thanks.

ROGER I'll have to get up some questions . . . My grandma and I are supposed to go to the village to have supper and go to a show . . . so there's no time now. You're having lobster.

(*He makes a face*)

TED I like it.

ROGER Ugh . . . Were you in the war?

TED Yes. I started on a destroyer off Guadalcanal . . . I see that name doesn't register with you.

ROGER No. We haven't studied American History yet. (TED *laughs*) What's funny?

TED I just hadn't thought of myself as part of history yet.

ROGER My dad was in the war, but he won't talk about it.

TED Well, he was quite a hero.

ROGER Mom has shown me his medals, but he won't talk about it. (*Indicating the vodka*) You want some more?

TED Not just this minute.

ROGER I better find out what happened to Mom. Why don't you come down. It's at least cooler in the garden. You're gonna eat out there . . . All the mosquitoes.

TED (*Sensing that something is wrong because* BARBARA *hasn't put in an appearance since he's arrived*) Maybe I'd better wait up here until—

ROGER (*Starting down*) No, come on.

TED (*Holding up his jacket*) What's the uniform going to be? Any idea?

ROGER I don't know. It's just gonna be you and Mom . . . I'll go get her. Maybe she needs to be zipped up or something. (*And he runs off to the house.* TED *frowns at what seems to be a "situation" arising. He goes to his suitcase, which is open on the bed, takes out a little package wrapped in tissue paper, and then slings his jacket over his shoulder, and picking up the tray with one hand, starts down the stairs.* ROGER, *entering the kitchen*) What's keeping Mom?

MRS. WALKER (*Feeling herself the victor*) I don't think she's feeling well. I don't think she's coming down.

ROGER She was getting dressed.

MRS. WALKER Was she? Well, she's probably changed her mind. I'll serve Mr. Sears his supper. (ROGER *starts up the stairs*) Roger, don't you disturb your mother.

ROGER (*Ignores this and goes to his mother's door, quietly*) Mom?

53

MRS. WALKER (*Calling up a rebuke*) Roger!

BARBARA Yes, Roger?

ROGER Can I come in?

BARBARA (*After a moment*) Yes, Roger.

ROGER (*Enters her room*) Aren't you coming down?

BARBARA (*Has picked up a comb before he enters*) I'm not quite ready yet, dear. You know I take forever.

ROGER I think you look great.

BARBARA Thank you. Have you been entertaining Mr. Sears?

ROGER He's nifty.

BARBARA (*Combing her hair*) You like him?

ROGER He's like you said he was.

BARBARA I don't remember saying anything about how he was.

ROGER When you came back from New York that time.

54

BARBARA (*Concerned*) I don't remember saying anything special about him ... Did you return the recorder?

ROGER Yes.

BARBARA Good.

ROGER (*Moves something in his mother's hairdo*) You looked better with it the other way.

BARBARA (*Nervous*) Did I?

ROGER You're just ruining it.

BARBARA Yes, I guess I am.

ROGER (*Looking out the window*) He's going to let me interview him.

BARBARA Good. Why don't you go down and do some of that ... and I'll ... I'll try to finish up here.

ROGER It looks as though Grandma's going to serve him his supper.

BARBARA What?
  (*She looks over his shoulder*)

MRS. WALKER (*Has come out to the garden, carrying a plate*)
Mr. Sears?

TED (*Coming over from where he's been sitting on the steps
to the barn*) Yes?

MRS. WALKER   I'm Barbara's mother, Mrs. Walker.

TED   How do you do?

MRS. WALKER   I'm so sorry nobody was available to greet
you this afternoon, but my daughter hasn't been feeling
too well . . . this heat, and well, I'm afraid she feels she'd
be rather poor company this evening.

TED   Oh, I'm sorry.
        (BARBARA, *in the bedroom, turns away from the win-
        dow, her eyes closed*)

MRS. WALKER   But since everything's all ready, I'll serve
you.

TED   Oh, no. I'm afraid I'm being a great trouble here.
        (TED *is confused now. There is obviously something
        going on that he doesn't understand*)

MRS. WALKER (*Going back into the kitchen*) It's no
trouble.

56

BARBARA (*Makes her decision, and comes quickly out of the room and down the stairs. An attempt at airiness*) Mother, I'm all ready now. I'll take over.

MRS. WALKER (*Cold*) I thought you were going to stay upstairs.

BARBARA (*Ignoring it, trying to stay pleasant, but is very nervous*) You and Roger can go in to the movies now.

MRS. WALKER No.

BARBARA Yes, Mother. You won't have much time.

MRS. WALKER No. (ROGER *observes this battle between the women, but doesn't enter into it*) I'll fix Roger some supper right here. I don't feel like eating.
(MRS. WALKER *and* BARBARA *stare at each other for a moment, then* BARBARA *turns away and goes outside to greet* TED)

BARBARA (*Very much on edge, but she tries to be casual and "social." It is obvious from the way she looks at him, in darting glances, that this is a meaningful encounter.* TED *also looks at her and talks to her in a way that reveals that he is searching for something more than is in their conversation*) Ted, I'm sorry to have all this confusion. How are you?
(*She shakes hands with him*)

TED   I'm fine. I'm afraid I'm very much in the way.

BARBARA   No. It's just that I was in the tub when you
    arrived, and then I . . . tore my dress getting into it, and
    . . . anyway, how are you?

TED   Good.

BARBARA   (*Going on*)   I didn't get a chance to get the room
    fixed up properly.

TED   It's great. But I must be putting someone out.

BARBARA   No. I fixed it up for David for a writing room, but
    he prefers to work in the attic. I don't know why. I some-
    times think he wants to be somewhere where he can be
    disturbed.
        (*She laughs at this idea*)

TED   How is David?

BARBARA   Oh, fine. He's taking the summer off from teach-
    ing, you know . . . to finally get his book written.

TED   I envy him.

BARBARA   He worked like a Trojan all term to make some
    extra loot so he could write this summer . . . Anyway, he's

pounding away. He said today he thought he had it licked.

TED   Good. Will he be there to heckle me at the conference?

BARBARA   No. His sacred work. You know. This is a big event, this book. Slightly terrifying, actually . . . first book in over ten years. His students ganged up and gave him a new typewriter, and a silver cup to hold his pencils.

TED   Driving up this afternoon, through that wonderful country, I said to myself, "This is what you ought to do . . . knock off the rat race and settle down some place like this and teach."

BARBARA (*Laughing*)   Oh, no. Really?

TED   Yes. Only I wouldn't be very good at it. I'm no good as a teacher. I tried once.

BARBARA   David's great, but he hates it. There you are. (*She realizes she has been rattling on, and she is flustered. They look at each other for a moment, till she finds the next subject*) Thank you for the lovely flowers.

TED   Oh, did they arrive?

59

BARBARA   I was in the village and the florist came out and asked me what I'd like. I hope I didn't do a terrible thing, but I asked for stock, because I knew it was Meg's favorite.

TED   That was nice.

BARBARA   I didn't know, really . . . you know . . . if you'd want to, well . . . anything for your anniversary.

TED   (*Looks at her for a long moment, takes a drink*)   I'd planned to go to the cemetery. But when I woke up this morning, some instinct . . . of self-preservation? . . . I don't know, but some instinct brought me up here.

BARBARA   (*Is puzzled by this, then*)   I shouldn't have chosen the stock then.

TED   No . . . no. For some strange reason, it's absolutely right . . . (*She looks at him, confused*) Can I make you a drink?

BARBARA   No . . . Oh, maybe some wine later with supper, but I haven't had a drink in—a—oh, a year. Nothing ominous about that . . . I just haven't.

TED   It seems to me you drank when we went out in New York.

BARBARA   Did I? . . . No, I don't think so. That's . . . well, that's about the time I stopped. (*There is an awkward pause*) I'm sorry I couldn't get down for the funeral. If you don't want to talk about Meg, just shut me up.

TED   No. No, really.

BARBARA   I just couldn't swing coming to the funeral. I suppose it sounds funny to you that someone can't swing a trip to New York, but anyway . . .

TED   Thank you for your letter.

BARBARA   Oh, I can't write letters. I can't even spell a word over one syllable. Yesterday I even spelled "those" t—h—o—e—s.

TED   It was a wonderful letter.

BARBARA (*Bothered by the intensity of this*) Oh?

TED   I carried it with me for months. All over Europe.

BARBARA   But why?

TED   It made me feel good. Most people wrote me how wonderful Meg was . . . which she was. You wrote me about how wonderful our marriage had seemed to you . . . and how . . . kind I'd been to her. It made me feel a little less guilty.

BARBARA   Guilty?

TED   Yes. The survivor is always the sinner.

BARBARA   But I've never seen anyone more devoted than you were.

TED (*He looks at her with appreciation*) Thanks . . . You look lovely. Your hair. It's nice.

BARBARA I usually slop around here like an old hag. But then I remembered you like your ladies to look like ladies.

TED Makes me sound rather grim.

BARBARA You said something about the way ladies should look when we went shopping for that bed jacket for Meg.

TED Did I?

BARBARA I don't think I ever thanked you properly for how kind you and Meg were to me when I was in New York.

TED You looked as though you needed someone to be kind to you.

BARBARA (*Guarded*) Did I?

TED I had the feeling you had something you wanted to bust out with . . . only you never got the chance . . . listening to me talk about Meg. I apologize.

BARBARA I thank you for letting me be so close to you and Meg for that week. I know it was a terrible time for both of you, with her so sick . . . but in a strange way I found it wonderfully—inspiring, watching you and her. I fell in love with your marriage. That's a funny thing to say, but I did.

TED It's a lovely thing to say.

BARBARA I can't explain it, but it sustained me for months. (*She is embarrassed; she has gone too far*) You look tired.

TED Yes, I am.

BARBARA We've followed your wanderings . . . in the papers.

TED To be more exact and less kind . . . in the gossip columns.

BARBARA (*With compassion*) Well . . .

TED That's so touching.

BARBARA What?

TED Your "well."

BARBARA I don't understand.

TED I came here tonight—for so many reasons I'm not quite sure of—but I think one of them was to hear you say "well."

BARBARA (*Is embarrassed by the intimacy of the conversation, and frightened. She goes to the kitchen, where* MRS. WALKER *has been fussing with some other food, and* ROGER *has been sitting on the steps*) I thought we'd eat outside tonight, because it's so hot.

63

TED   That's fine.

BARBARA (*When she gets inside, she stands for a moment. She is frankly afraid now.* TED *is obviously striking a more personal level than she can cope with. She looks at her mother*)   Mother, will you bring out the lobster?

MRS. WALKER (*Ominously*)   You see?

BARBARA   Roge, I know you don't like lobster, but if you'd like to join us...

MRS. WALKER   We'll have something in here.

ROGER   Aren't we going to the movies?

BARBARA   Maybe tomorrow night.
(ROGER *goes to his room. She gets the bottle of wine and starts out*)

TED   Is David going to join us?

BARBARA   Maybe later. But he's gone to his office to work. He sometimes escapes to a cubbyhole he has at the English Department . . . I apologize for the wine ahead of time. We don't have much selection up here, and it's probably all wrong.
(*She hands it to him to pour*)

64

TED   Looks fine.

(He is constantly observing BARBARA, *trying to figure out why she is so keyed up, trying to bring her down to normal.* MRS. WALKER *brings out the plate of lobster)*

BARBARA   Once David and I were entertaining some faculty, and I made a huge lobster salad, and I'd laid in a little tongue also . . . just in case. *(She laughs)* Before dinner I asked David to ask the guests if by any *chance,* there was anyone who didn't like lobster. There was a terrible moment of polite silence, and then one by one they all, and I mean *all,* murmured, "If there is anything else." There wasn't enough tongue, so the more hardy had the salad, and there was much discreet pushing of unwanted pieces of lobster under large lettuce leaves. For years David and I laughed about that. "Is there anyone here who by chance doesn't like lobster?"

TED   Well, I love it.

BARBARA   I remember you had it Newburgh when we went out. But I thought it was so hot . . .

TED   Nice eye. Very observant. Thanks.

BARBARA   Perhaps you'd prefer beer with it. Beer isn't exactly as festive, but I do have it.

TED   No. This is just right.

BARBARA (*Jabbering on*) I tried to get all knuckles and claws, because that's the most tender part, but I couldn't.

TED Wine?

BARBARA Oh ... Yes, all right. Thank you.

TED (*Lifts his glass*) Well ...

BARBARA Yes ... to ... well ...
      (*They understand they are drinking to Meg and the marriage*)

TED I've brought you a small present.

BARBARA Oh, nothing more. Please.

TED It's nothing.

BARBARA (*Panicking*) Really, I don't want anything more. The flowers.

TED (*Taking the small box from his pocket*) It's a sentimental present. When you were in New York, I was very touched by your feelings about Meg.

BARBARA I told you I fell in love with your marriage.

TED   It's a pin of hers . . . It wasn't something I gave her
. . . something she had before I met her.

BARBARA   I couldn't. (*She is deeply moved; this threatens
the social face she has tried to put on*) I'm not good at
accepting things. I never have been.

TED   I know. I'm not either, but—
(*He holds it out again to her*)

BARBARA (*Moves away from the table quickly*)   No.

TED   Barbara . . .

BARBARA (*Starts to cry*)   I'm sorry.
(*She runs into the kitchen and upstairs to her room,
and sits on the bed, not sobbing, but crying because
of the tension of the situation, and because she is
touched by his simple gesture.* TED *is puzzled; he
moves away from the table to the barn stairs, picks up
the drink he had left there, and looks at the house. In
a few moments,* DAVID *appears in the kitchen, having
come in through a front door*)

MRS. WALKER (*Looks at him, afraid*)   Oh, David.

DAVID (*Is subdued, serious*)   I thought you and Roger were
going to the movies.

MRS. WALKER (*Willing to leave now, to get* ROGER *away from what she fears is to follow*) Yes . . . yes, we are. Barbara's upstairs . . . I was serving Mr. Sears his supper.

DAVID Take Roger and go to the movies.
(*He goes upstairs to his study, and during the following, puts the top on the typewriter, gets a couple of notebooks, and, carrying them, starts down the stairs to his bedroom*)

MRS. WALKER Yes . . . yes . . . (*She goes outside*) Mr. Sears, I'm terribly sorry—

TED Is she all right?

MRS. WALKER Yes . . . it's just that . . . well . . .

TED I'll go in town for dinner.
(*And he heads up the barn stairs*)

MRS. WALKER Oh, would you? Thank you.
(TED *goes into his room with his drink. He looks over to the house, wondering. He yanks some stuff out of a drawer, with the idea of packing, then he doesn't. During the following scene with* BARBARA *and* DAVID, *he goes down and away, leaving his suitcase open on the bed*)

MRS. WALKER (*Goes to* ROGER'S *room from the garden*) Come along, Roger. We're going to the movies.

ROGER   What?

MRS. WALKER   Your father's home. They want to be alone.
Now come along.

ROGER   I don't understand.

MRS. WALKER   (*Going downstairs, having taken her purse
from her room*)   There's nothing to understand. We're
just going to the movies.

ROGER   (*As they reach the garden*)   Where's Mr. Sears?

MRS. WALKER   He's going into the village to eat.
(*And she walks off.* ROGER *follows, looking around,
troubled and bewildered.* BARBARA *has been aware of*
DAVID *going up the stairs. She waits, expectantly,
fearfully*)

DAVID   (*Comes down the stairs with the typewriter. He
pauses outside the door, then goes in. He looks at the floor,
then at her*)   I'm sorry for the—
(*With a gesture he indicates the violence downstairs*)

BARBARA   (*Still tentative*)   It's all right. It was my fault. I
didn't—

DAVID   No. It's incredible that I could—
(*He can't go into it*)

69

BARBARA   It doesn't matter.

DAVID   It does! It's despicable. And I'm tired of being despicable.

BARBARA (*A note of tenderness*)   Oh, David.

DAVID   No, please! Don't be kind. Don't be understanding. I don't want your understanding and patience and self-sacrifice . . . any more. I can't stand the burden of it.

BARBARA   Why should it be a burden?

DAVID   I have hurt you. For years I have hurt you.

BARBARA   No.

DAVID   Yes! And because I have hurt you, I have come to hate you.

BARBARA   You haven't hurt me.

DAVID (*Desperate*)   Let's not lie, Barbara! I have lied to myself for years, that even if everything else has gone wrong, I have been a good husband and have not hurt anyone but myself. But the truth is I have hurt . . . everyone. I have been a coward. Beware of gentle, weak men who don't want to hurt anyone. They haven't the courage to make a clean, cutting, killing decision. But they will

anyway, with dragged-out murdering compromises . . .
until everyone—and everything—is dead. I loved you,
Barbara. Believe that. Know that. I loved you. But now
I must go away.

(*He drags out a suitcase*)

BARBARA   No.

DAVID   I can't tell you for how long I've wanted to go . . . to
disappear, to find four bare walls, a chair, a table, and
work! Each time I've seen the picture of the inside of an
artist's studio, I've become so excited, I've almost been
sick. When I read of artists wandering the face of the
earth alone, living on their work, in their work, going mad
with their work—Van Gogh cutting off his ear, Gauguin
setting sail for Tahiti—I have been sick with an inde-
scribable longing . . . Oh, Barbara, I want to write from
morn to midnight and midnight to morn. And if I eat, it
will be because I am a writer . . . and if I die, it will be
because I am a writer. Fifteen years ago, on a beach, when
everything was promises and beginnings, I said something
like this to you—and we both soared on the words—and
then . . .

BARBARA   I did it, didn't I?

DAVID   Oh, God, no, Barbara. I did it. I loved you so. I
wanted to make you so proud of me. I wanted to be everything I saw I was in your eyes. I didn't want to be this
nothing . . . this failure.

BARBARA   You are not a failure. You are a great teacher.

DAVID   Who hates and envies his students. For years I have
fired them with a burning passion . . . evenings I have
talked to them down there . . . about purity, integrity,
commitment to one's art . . . and they have gone out of the
house flying, inspired, and I have come up here to bed and
ground my teeth in frustration. Barbara, I have to do this.

BARBARA   I'll work, David. I'll go back to work and you
can—

DAVID   No. We tried that. Again, it is my fault. I don't
seem to be able to . . . do that. Others can, I know. I can't.

BARBARA   Oh, David.

DAVID   Barbara, don't.

BARBARA   Go, if you have to . . . for a little while. See.

DAVID (*Stuffing things into his suitcase*)   No.

BARBARA   Oh, yes.

DAVID   No. It can't be that way. I don't know why, but it
needs . . . an act of tearing . . . a cruel act, an act of commitment. Something clear and irrevocable. It cannot be

with permission, with sanction . . . on a let's-see basis.
(BARBARA *cries softly*) Oh, God, you never should have
listened to me, Barbara. I never should have spoken. I've
betrayed us both . . . (*He comes to her tenderly*) Barbara,
you're losing nothing. Are you crying because there'll
be no more fights? Are you crying because you'll miss my
coming home drunk at night and raping you?

BARBARA Don't!

DAVID Why not? It's the truth.

BARBARA No.

DAVID That's what it's been. Don't lie to yourself. Rape!

BARBARA It has not been.

DAVID It has. I come home torn with tensions and anxieties
and needs. But I am so full of bitterness and resentment
for you—a resentment and bitterness I am ashamed of,
but they are there—and I can't come near you until I am
drunk. And then it is rape. And I am tired of raping my
wife.

BARBARA How can you say that?

DAVID Because it's the truth. And I want you to know what
it is we have here. When is the last time you wanted me?
Who can remember!

73

BARBARA That's not true.

DAVID Barbara, darling. I have not been deceived by your pretended joys . . . your sweet, generous little cries of joy. They have only made me despise myself more.

BARBARA Oh, David, I have loved just holding you in my arms. It doesn't have to be—

DAVID Oh, Barbara, don't.

BARBARA I can want you. But you came to me drunk. I knew you had to come to me drunk, and I didn't think you wanted me . . . unless you were drunk, and I . . . Oh, David . . .

DAVID You cried this afternoon at my letter. And I knew why. Not because that man was coming, but because I wanted to sweep you off to one of our masquerade nights when we used to be able to make everything right with the world by one night in bed . . . and you couldn't. And I can't either any more, without the bottle, because I become impotent with failure and resentment.

BARBARA Oh, David, what can I do?

DAVID (*After a pause*) Nothing.
(*He starts to close his suitcase*)

BARBARA We have so much.

74

DAVID   We have nothing . . . If I thought I was going to measure out my life in examination books and dedications and . . . and crud . . . I'd kill myself right now.

BARBARA (*Not looking at him, barely getting it out*)   My father left my mother—and overnight her hair turned white. (DAVID *looks at her, stricken*) I didn't mean to say that. But I'm afraid.

DAVID (*Comes to where she is sitting, and touches her*) Barbara . . . oh, listen to me, Barbara. I would like to say so many things I . . . mustn't say. Barbara, you are lovely, you are beautiful, you are strong . . . Don't be afraid. (*With difficulty*) I shall envy and hate the man you come to love.
      (*He moves away from her quickly, to his suitcase*)

BARBARA (*Encouraged by the tender tone of his voice*) David.

DAVID   No, Barbara.

BARBARA (*After a moment, in a sudden flare-up*)   All right . . . go away. Get out! Get out!

DAVID (*Winces at this but takes his suitcase and typewriter, and starts down the stairs*)   Goodbye, Barbara.

BARBARA (*Springs after him, at the top of the stairs*)   David . . . I'm afraid.

DAVID (*Stops, in the kitchen, not facing her*) I'm afraid too, Barbara. I'm terrified, that if I stayed, I would kill you ... I would kill us both.

(*Without looking back, he hurries out the door and is gone.*

BARBARA *stands staring down the stairs—in a state of despair and shock—as the lights dim out on her, and on the area over the barn, and* TED's *half-packed suitcase*)

Curtain

Act Two

Scene One

It is about an hour later. BARBARA *is in the bedroom. She is standing before a mirror brushing her hair back perfunctorily. She is still dazed and her actions are slow. She slips into a cardigan, and then sits on the bed, staring at her hands. Her gaze wanders in the direction of the barn; there is no light there. Slowly she wanders downstairs. She looks at the things still left around from the unserved supper. She puts a few things away. She goes outside and clears the platter from the table, looks at the food, and puts it aside. She sits again and just stares. After a few moments,* TED *comes into the garden. He stands in the beam of light coming out the door and just looks at her. She doesn't see him, as she stares in front of her.*

TED (*Very gently*) Barbara?

BARBARA Oh.
    (*She slowly gets up and opens the screen door for him*)

TED I started to pack to leave . . . and then I didn't. I'm afraid I'm in the—

BARBARA Oh, no.

TED   I walked into the village and around the campus. Very nostalgic.
(*In spite of the casualness of what he says, he keeps looking at* BARBARA, *trying to find out what's happened*)

BARBARA   Did you get anything to eat?

TED   I didn't really feel like it.

BARBARA   But you've been all day—

TED   Yes, I know. Did you eat?

BARBARA   No. I think the lobster's been out too long. (*With a smile*) There may be some tongue.

TED   No, thanks. It's too hot.

BARBARA   Yes. Silly to have a sweater on. But I felt cold. Make yourself a drink.

TED   You?

BARBARA   Maybe some of the wine. (*She goes out to the garden, where the wine is still on the table.* TED *follows her in a moment*) A fine anniversary dinner for you.

TED   I'm afraid I had no business coming here. I wanted
to desperately . . . (*She looks at him, and he pauses a
moment*) but I had no business coming.

BARBARA   You were invited.

TED   I invited myself.

BARBARA   I said "Yes."

TED   But David.

BARBARA   He said "Yes." You heard him.

TED   Yes, I heard him. And I thought of going to the Inn
when I heard him. *But still I came.* Then when Roger met
me, there wasn't much I could do . . . and then suddenly—

BARBARA   Yes . . . David has gone off for a few days . . . to
get some of his writing done. He thinks—(*She stops for
a long moment*) Oh, what's the sense of lying to you?
Why am I afraid to tell you the truth? He's gone . . .
away. Away. Not just for a few days.
(*She turns from him*)

TED   I'm sorry.
(*He makes a move to touch her*)

BARBARA (*Afraid of his touch, she moves away*) No, please.

TED It's my fault.

BARBARA Oh, no. If it hadn't been . . . it would have been something else. It's been that way . . . This book, this book which is going to change our lives. He's been writing a book for ten years which is going to make everything different.
(*Her handkerchief goes to her face*)

TED (*Again, comforting*) Barbara.

BARBARA I think I'd better go in.

TED Why? (BARBARA *looks at him; she is afraid of his comfort*) Please don't.

BARBARA I don't want to be disgusting. My God, Meg died without a tear, without a whimper. And I—

TED Meg cried.

BARBARA But she didn't make a public display . . . David wants to be free. He wants to fly—to write from morn to midnight, and midnight to morn—to cut off his ear and sail for Tahiti with . . . Gauguin.

TED   I see.

BARBARA   He wants to be free. And I don't blame him. I have done a terrible thing to him.

TED   What?

BARBARA   It's my fault this second book has never been written.

TED   Now, Barbara.

BARBARA   It is. Fifteen years ago, when we first met, he was a kid back from the war, a hero with medals for bravery, for being shot up, for being sunk. People just wanted to touch him. He came back a kid and a hero, and I turned him into a middle-aged man and a bum.

TED   Nobody turns anyone into anything.

BARBARA   Oh, but I did. Very gradually and very completely. We met after the war, when he came back to study under the G.I. Bill. And he wrote his book, a small experience he'd had in the war, and he read it to me as it went along . . . and I cried and laughed and told him how wonderfully he wrote, and the book was published, and that was the catastrophe of our lives.

TED   But you had nothing to do with that.

BARBARA   I thought he wanted to be a writer, just to be a
writer. I didn't know then that it was his only way out of
a dreary world he finds impossible . . . I should have
known, though, because when we were courting, we'd go
to the beach weekends, and city families would come
down loaded with picnic kits, blankets and umbrellas . . .
and he'd look at them and say, "If I thought I'd ever spend
my life like that, I'd quit right now." And of course I said,
"You won't have to. You're brilliant." No one had ever
loved me before. I was not, am not, pretty or beautiful.
But he loved what he called the interesting planes in my
face, and my eyes. He always insisted they were violet
when they're blue. And in return for loving me, I wanted
to give him a gift he seemed to want so desperately . . .
that he could be a brilliant success, and would not have to
come dragging the family to the beach, like everyone else
. . . And we were married and descended on Mecca—
New York, New York. And then, nothing. He could have
gotten along on peanut butter sandwiches by himself. But
he was a gentleman and couldn't stand to see me starve.
And my getting a job as a receptionist didn't work. It
killed him taking money from me on Fridays. I'd try to
avoid handing it to him. I'd try to leave it on a table with
a note, and then stay out till he'd come in and picked it
up. But it didn't work, so he got this job teaching up here
—planning to write evenings and weekends. From then
on he has had an excuse for not writing. And I did it with
my little bow and arrow.

TED   Barbara, a lot of writers have taught and still made it.

BARBARA   Oh, yes, and I know all their names. I went to a library and got out a *Who's Who of Authors,* and I listed all the famous writers who had taught and written on the side. I used to bring out their names, one at a time, for encouragement. But finally it didn't encourage him. It made him furious, and I stopped.

TED   I . . . I hate him for letting you think it's your fault. But I understand it too.

BARBARA   "To my darling wife, without whom I could not have written this book." If we accept that, we must also be willing to accept, "With whom I could not write this damned book." It's a damned book now.

TED   Most books are before they're finished.

BARBARA   After three years I went away on some pretext. He didn't know I was planning not to come back. I was ruining his life, and I couldn't stand it. But his letters were so full of need, so loving . . . The letter he wrote me tonight . . . It breaks your heart . . . And I came back . . . And later, I tricked him into having a child he didn't want. I knew it was cruel, but I couldn't wait any longer for his "tomorrow" when it would have been fine to have a child. So I had Roger . . . You didn't have any children.

TED   We wanted them. We couldn't have them.

BARBARA   I'm so sorry . . . We had them to kill. (TED *looks at her, not understanding*) You said about my visit to

85

New York, it seemed I had something I wanted to talk about. That was it. I went to New York to get rid of a child that was starting in me. (TED *makes an instinctive move to comfort her*) No, please, don't, or I will have to shut up, and I don't want to shut up. I told my mother, I wanted you to come . . . so that I could talk to you.

TED Thank you.

BARBARA Somewhere, deep inside me, is a scream. I hope I won't scream. If I talk, perhaps I won't scream. My mother screamed. My father screamed. I have never screamed . . . yet.

TED I wouldn't mind.

BARBARA But I would. Did Meg scream? No, I didn't ask that question. I don't want to know if she did or didn't. How horrified she would have been—me sitting by her bed, holding her hand, and just having killed my child.

TED She wouldn't have been horrified . . . Sad, but not horrified.

BARBARA I wanted another child before it was too late. But when I knew I was going to have it, I panicked and came to New York. I stopped drinking then. I was afraid what would happen if I had a drink.

TED   I feel so guilty . . . It makes no sense, I suppose, but I feel so guilty.

BARBARA   Why?

TED   As a man, I feel guilty.

BARBARA   He didn't do it. He knew nothing about it. My mother had taken sick and come to live with us by then . . . How could I give him another mouth to feed. No wonder he wants to be free. And I am terrified of it.

TED   His freedom?

BARBARA   No, mine.

TED   Oh.

BARBARA   Why did you say "his freedom"?

TED   (*Not wanting to go into it*)   What is there to fear in yours?

BARBARA   (*After a moment*)   For fifteen years David has been the condition of my life . . . the reference point for all the love, ambition, hope and guilt. (TED *nods his head*) It's not easy to . . .

TED   No.

BARBARA And . . . When I was eight, one night my father walked out the front door and never came back. My mother went into her room and didn't come out till two days later. When she did, her hair was white.

TED Mmmmm.

BARBARA This was the world David came into . . . a hero riding his bicycle with an outrageous red scarf flying out behind. His personal banner of defiance against the drabness of the world. (*She smiles*) When David was a kid—he was a slum kid, living with his aunt—he came home one day with this piece of silk he'd found some place . . . and he hung it up over the bed he shared with his two cousins . . . and he'd lie there for hour after hour looking at it, dreaming God knows what. He took it to war with him. It was his promise to me that my marriage would not be like my mother's—a promise of ecstasy . . . eternal passion . . . eternal unreality.

TED (*After a long moment*) Do you still love him?

BARBARA (*Impatiently turns away*) Oh.

TED I'm sorry. That's an impertinent question.

BARBARA No. I mean "No, don't be sorry." Why shouldn't you ask a wife if she loves her husband? It's a legitimate question. (*But she is not answering it.* TED *waits out the uncomfortable pause*) David and I . . . just are. Oh, that sounds so belittling. I didn't mean that. But how can I answer?

TED   I understand.

BARBARA   My mother says I should be afraid. This seems cheap to me to hang on to a man because you're afraid . . . to be alone, or afraid that no man will ever love you again. She says with a child of ten— A man courted her when my father left but, I don't know—something happened. And she was pretty. She says a woman does anything to get away from loneliness. You've known many women. And that's true, I suppose. Isn't it?

TED   It's true of men too.

BARBARA   Yes. And is he ashamed afterwards? Is he ashamed of the women he has been with for loneliness? You were.

TED   I?

BARBARA   You seemed to imply that.

TED   Not ashamed, no. Not at all. Immensely grateful.

BARBARA   You would be. I think a woman knows that about you. Certainly if she had seen you with Meg . . . What would she have done if you had died? Would she have gone to Europe? Would she have?

TED I don't know.

BARBARA I imagine it can be terrible. I had a friend whose husband died—about my age. It's grotesque, but soon after he died, she thought she was being eaten alive by mites. Little almost invisible insects. She clawed and scraped at herself, and when no doctor could find any mites on her, she collected these little things in a jar to show him they were real. They were only little specks of dust . . . (*She suddenly blurts out*) I am terrified of that kind of freedom!
    (*She covers her face with her hands, and moves to the house.* TED *is moving after her*)

MRS. WALKER (*Comes from the back, above the barn*) Barbara. (BARBARA *continues into the house*) Mr. Sears. (TED *nods, but looks towards* BARBARA. MRS. WALKER *assumes her best manners*) I wonder if we could be excused for a few minutes?
    (TED *moves over to the barn steps and sits, but his attention is very much on the house.* MRS. WALKER *enters the kitchen*)

BARBARA Where is Roger?

MRS. WALKER Next door. We met Peter on the way home, and he's over there having ice cream. I wanted to talk to you alone. Could we go upstairs?

BARBARA Mother, I don't want to talk about anything. Please.

(MRS. WALKER, *with a determined look on her face,
simply stands and indicates the stairs.* BARBARA *looks
at her—puzzled at the look on her face—and slowly
goes upstairs to her room*)

MRS. WALKER (*As she follows* BARBARA) What happened
when Roger and I left? (BARBARA *turns as though she
would scream if anyone asked her anything more*) I have
a right to know.

BARBARA (*Going into her room*) I will tell you, but I won't
rake it back and forth, back and forth. David has gone.
He wants to be free, to work, to write. That's what he's
always wanted. I've stood in his way, and now he's gone.
He's free.

MRS. WALKER He's down in his office in the English Department. (BARBARA *looks at her mother, waiting for
whatever else she has to say, not surprised*) As we came
along after the movies, I saw a light in the building, in his
office . . . Roger was ahead with Peter, so I just went up
the walk and looked in.
  (*She waits for effect*)

BARBARA (*Explodes*) Oh, come on. What is it?

MRS. WALKER You said there was no girl. (BARBARA *looks
at her sharply*) Oh, my baby. (BARBARA *moves away*)
Nancy—you know her.

BARBARA   She's just one of his students.

MRS. WALKER   Well, she was in his office with him.

BARBARA (*Is obviously hurt badly, but she covers*)   She sometimes does typing for him ... often.

MRS. WALKER   They were having a drink. (BARBARA *turns away*) Oh, my baby.

BARBARA   Mother, don't.

MRS. WALKER   You used to hold me when I was in trouble.

BARBARA   I don't want to be held.

MRS. WALKER   Please take my advice now.

BARBARA (*Opening her purse*)   Mother, here are the keys to the car ... and some money. (*She dumps out all her money*) I want you to take Roger to the Lake for a day or two.

MRS. WALKER   Tomorrow.

BARBARA   Tonight. Now.

MRS. WALKER   What are you going to do?

BARBARA   I just want to be absolutely alone.

MRS. WALKER *(Suddenly gloves off)*   With him ... Do you think he'll marry you?

BARBARA   Mother, shut up. What the hell are you talking about?

MRS. WALKER   Do you want to know why Ralph didn't marry me? (BARBARA *can't follow her, shakes her head*) He didn't marry me because he didn't want to marry a woman with a child. He married a girl young enough to be his daughter. They all do.

BARBARA   I'm sorry, Mother.

MRS. WALKER   I don't want you to be sorry. I want you to listen to me.

BARBARA   I want to be alone.

MRS. WALKER   Forget your pride and go down to David.

BARBARA   Go, Mother.

MRS. WALKER   This man is an adventurer ... you know that. You've read the papers.

BARBARA   On your way out say good night to Mr. Sears for me.

MRS. WALKER (*Comes closer to her*)   Barbara?

BARBARA   Mother?

MRS. WALKER   What are you going to do? I don't like the way you're talking!

BARBARA (*Throws it at her*)   Take all the knives and razors and sleeping pills if you want.

MRS. WALKER (*Shocked at her manner*)   Barbara, we've always been able to talk.

BARBARA   We have never said a meaningful thing to each other in our lives. We have never been able to talk . . . I have not been able to talk with anyone . . . except a stranger.
　　(*She waves towards* TED)

MRS. WALKER   Oh, Barbara, you make me feel so useless.

BARBARA   I'm sorry, Mother.

MRS. WALKER   I can't leave you like this.

94

Can one relationship contain everything?
Can a love built on/around joy and
　　happiness, in those terms, also
　　　contain sorrow and suffering?

BARBARA   Do you want to stay and hear me say more? Because I'm going to say more, presently.

MRS. WALKER   (*Looking at the keys and money on the table*) This is all you have.

BARBARA   It doesn't matter.

MRS. WALKER   Barbara?

BARBARA   (*Like an animal, turns on her*)   Get out!
   (MRS. WALKER *is terrified, and takes the keys and money, and goes to her room to get a few things.* BARBARA, *alone at last, flops on the bed and stares at the ceiling*)

ROGER   (*Has entered, eating an ice-cream cone, and has heard "Get out." He stops and looks up at the window, and frowns, turns from the house and sees* TED *on the steps*)   Hi.

TED   Hi.

ROGER   (*Embarrassed for his family*)   Kind of noisy.

TED   Your mother and your grandmother.

ROGER   Oh . . . You want an ice-cream cone?

TED   No, thanks.

ROGER   My friend makes them next door.

TED (*Shows* ROGER *his drink*)   Oh, yeah?
            (*They stay like this for a moment, then*)

ROGER   Where's my father?

TED   He's off working . . . somewhere else.

ROGER   Did he go to the Lake?

TED   I don't know.

ROGER   We got this cottage—it's not ours. Friends of ours
have it and they're away for the summer . . . I thought
maybe he'd gone there.

TED   How was the movie?

ROGER (*Gives his cone considerable attention from time to
time*)   It was a war movie.

TED   Which war?

ROGER   It wasn't knights and things like that. It was, I
guess, your war.

TED   Oh.

ROGER   Had some real shots of . . . uh . . . kami-something
or other.

TED (*His real interest is still on the house*)   Kamikazes . . .
suicide planes . . . Probably Okinawa.

ROGER   Yeah. Were you there?

TED   Yes. So was your dad.

ROGER   Did those guys really slam into those ships like that.
Bam—bam—bam!

TED   Your dad's ship was sunk there.

ROGER   It was? He never talks about it.

TED   Maybe some day when you study American History,
you'll read about The Fleet That Came to Stay.

MRS. WALKER (*Has come out into the garden*)   Roger. Oh,
Roger, your mother wants you to put a few things in a
bag. We're going to the Lake.

ROGER (*To* TED)   You'll see the Lake.

MRS. WALKER No. Just you and me.

ROGER Aw!

MRS. WALKER Now, Roger.

ROGER (*Heads towards the house*) Mom ...

MRS. WALKER Roger! You mustn't bother your mother. She's not feeling well ... and she's gone to bed. Now do as I say. You have a lot of things at the Lake already, so just get your toothbrush and whatever you'll need.

ROGER How long we gonna be there?

MRS. WALKER I don't know ... just a day or two. (ROGER, *puzzled, drifts off and upstairs, where he pauses in front of his mother's room for a moment, then goes into his own room and puts a toothbrush and a few things in a canvas bag. After an embarrassed moment or two between* MRS. WALKER *and* TED, *she turns to him*) Mr. Sears, I'm very frightened.

TED About what, Mrs. Walker?

MRS. WALKER You know what's happened here, I'm sure.

TED Something of it.

98

MRS. WALKER It's a silly, routine family tiff, but Barbara's taken it very hard. She's tired, and the heat, and . . . It's embarrassing for me to talk this way to a stranger, but . . . Well, I'm being thrown out of the house. I'm leaving to avoid a violent scene . . . and I'm frightened.

TED About what?

MRS. WALKER I have no idea what Barbara might do—in the way of violence—to herself. Do you understand?

TED Yes.

MRS. WALKER I don't know what anyone can do. But I feel absolutely helpless.

ROGER (*Coming out with his small canvas satchel*) Shouldn't I say goodbye to Mom?

MRS. WALKER No.

ROGER (*Suddenly peevish*) Why do we have to go now? I was talking to him.

MRS. WALKER We just have to. Your mother wants us to.

TED We'll talk again, Roger.

ROGER You'll be gone when I come back.

TED   How far is the Lake?

ROGER   Half an hour.

TED   Maybe I'll come down tomorrow afternoon for a swim.

ROGER   Okay, and bring Mom. Is that a promise?

TED   It's not a promise, but I'll try.

MRS. WALKER   The telephone number is on the kitchen wall, incidentally.

TED   All right.
        (*He holds out his hand to Roger*)

ROGER (*Taking it and staring at the ground*)   Well . . .

TED   Take care of yourself.

ROGER (*Still hanging on to the hand*)   Yeah. (*After another long moment or two, he starts off*)   Well, so long.

TED   So long. (*To Mrs. Walker*) Good night.
        (MRS. WALKER *looks at him, worried both by him and the situation, but at last she leaves*)

BARBARA (*When she hears the voices stop, she breathes more easily. She sits up, on the side of the bed, and just stares for a moment. The added fact that there may be a girl has numbed her, and made everything seem futile. She reaches out and turns out the light. She plays aimlessly with the folds of her skirt, paying infinite attention to running her fingers up and down the creases. She is almost slack-jawed. She sees that there is still a light downstairs, and she raises herself and manages to get downstairs. She sees the bottle of whiskey, fingers it for a moment, and then pours herself a stiff drink—and drinks it. She clutches the bottle to her, and turns and is going up the stairs, when she sees* TED *standing in the door)* Please don't come in.

TED Why?

BARBARA Oh, don't ask questions, please. I want to be alone ... absolutely alone.

TED I won't ask questions. I'd just like to come in.
(BARBARA *shakes her head.* TED *comes in anyway*)

BARBARA (*Bitterly*) For someone who is supposed to be so understanding—

TED We were talking a few minutes ago.

BARBARA Yes.

TED You said that's why you asked me up here?

BARBARA There's nothing left to say. I just want to be
alone.

TED There are things I'd like to say.

BARBARA Oh, no. I don't want arguments.

TED Not arguments.

BARBARA I don't want anyone talking sense with me tonight. This is not the night for sense. This is a night for
. . . absurdity. So please. You want a drink. Here. (*She
pours a shot and hands it to him*) Now go.
        (TED *sits*)

BARBARA (*Rushes at him*) No. Go! Go!

TED (*Rising and trying to take her shoulders*) Barbara.
(BARBARA *pulls away*) What did your mother tell you
that's—

BARBARA Nothing extraordinary. She went peeping into
windows.

TED I see.

BARBARA And what she saw was nothing. (TED *shakes his
head, saddened*) I don't want to talk. You want me to talk.
You want me to dribble out this feeling—to—

TED (*Takes her by the shoulders*) What feeling?

BARBARA (*Almost yelling*) This feeling. Leave me alone.
Won't you leave me alone. (*She rushes up the stairs*) I
want to die. Can't you let me die.
> (*She goes into her bedroom, and crouches alongside
> the bed, like a small girl saying her prayers.* TED *fol-
> lows her quickly and alertly, but discreetly. He
> stands at the door watching her sobbing, then he
> comes in and sits down. He lights a cigarette, and
> bends over and touches her back gently, just to make
> contact.* BARBARA *draws further within herself*)

TED (*Ever so gently*) People should never believe us when
we say we want to be alone. We mean so much the opposite . . . We want someone to hold us . . . to love us.

BARBARA No.

TED But it always seems impossible that anyone could do
that . . . so we say, "I want to be alone."

BARBARA I want to die.
> (TED *doesn't say anything, he just is there*)

BARBARA (*After a few moments, relaxes a bit, and turns and
slumps, sitting on the floor, leaning against the bed*) I'm
tired . . . For years I've been tired. It's been like running
up and down a long hall keeping doors to ugly rooms shut
tight. Now I want them all to open . . . I don't care. I

want it all to come down. I just want to run whimpering into oblivion. (TED *holds his drink out to her. She takes a sip*) Oh, sweet Jesus. Is this it? Is this the way the world ends?

TED   Barbara?

BARBARA   Don't reason with me. I'm sick of reasoning with myself, my mother, my son. I only know what I feel in my blood . . . in my bones . . . Utter desolation.
(TED *takes one of her limp hands and holds it a moment*)

BARBARA (*Looking down at the clasped hands*)   What is this . . . the lifeline?

TED   Perhaps.

BARBARA   Why are you so determined to keep me alive?

TED   Because you don't really want to die, and if by accident you did . . . it would be terrible. You just want to—to go to the depths, and I respect that feeling.

BARBARA (*Yanks her hand away*)   I can't go there with you —you sitting there being understanding. I can only go there . . . in defiance. (*She rises*) David said, "I cannot let you *let* me go. I have to tear away . . ." to smash, to break. (*She throws her glass and smashes it, then laughs a humorless laugh*) So puny, so futile . . . Everything inside me is aching to snap—to explode—and I manage to break a glass. You see, I am not one of your ladies.

TED (*Stands*) Barbara.

BARBARA (*Standing tense now, as though she might leap from inside herself*) Please go. Get the hell out of here. I won't kill myself. I promise. But I want to do terrible things . . . I want to shout obscene words and . . . (*She opens her mouth to shout, but gags. He grabs her hand*) Let go of my hand. (*She yanks it loose*) Do I shock you?

TED No.

BARBARA What do I have to do to shock you? How far does your understanding and compassion go?

TED No matter where, I've been there before you.

BARBARA (*Spitting it out, as though to shock him*) I hate my son because he made my husband hate me.

TED Yes.

BARBARA I hate my mother because she taught me fear . . . because she had a heart attack and brought another mouth to feed . . . because she wants me to crawl . . . because she says I'd become a whore if I'm left alone . . . and

she's right. The nights I've lain in bed crying for an end
to desire. But it never comes. Never an end ... And I hate
myself, for hating what I should love.

(TED *comes to her very tenderly and takes her face
in his hands*)

BARBARA (*Not moving away, quietly*) Oh, God. Don't.

TED (*Very tenderly, close to her*) Barbara.

BARBARA Oh, God, no. Please don't let this happen. I
didn't want this to happen. (*But suddenly they are in a
tight embrace, she kissing him hungrily. Then her cheek
next to his, crying*) Oh, no.

TED (*Moves his face from hers for a moment to look at her.
She covers her face with her hands, and turns and kneels
by the bed again. He moves towards her*) Barbara ...

BARBARA (*Low*) No. (*Then suddenly a little cry*) Help!
(TED *stands looking down at her, wanting to hold her;
instead he turns quickly and goes downstairs. There, he
waits a moment, then quickly goes outside and disappears
beyond the barn.* BARBARA *remains crumpled up by the
bed for a long time. She is shattered by the full awareness
she now has of her desire for this man. She feels the
terrible longing openly now, and it frightens her.*

After a little time, DAVID *comes into the garden, tentatively, almost like a man coming to see something he does
not want to see. He has drunk quite a bit, but he is not*

*really drunk. He comes in and looks up the stairs and
stops there.* BARBARA *hears the footsteps, and she rises
from the floor and slowly goes to the door and looks down
the stairs. She is happy to see him. She comes down the
stairs towards him, but he moves away as she comes. She
stops and looks at the floor)*   Help me, David.

DAVID *(He is moved by her cry for help, but he doesn't
understand and doesn't want to understand)*   Your
mother—*(He stops.* BARBARA *looks up at him. It is difficult to say, he says it haltingly)* Your mother came by ...
She said you might ... *(He looks inquiringly at her for
a moment, makes a gesture with his hand, and looks at the
floor again)* She was afraid you'd ...
        (He stops)

BARBARA *(Looks at him a long time, then shakes her head)*
No.

DAVID *(Relieved and even grateful, but unable to express
it, shakes his head up and down)*   Jesus, don't.
        *(*BARBARA *shakes her head again and they look at
each other a moment.* DAVID *starts to go)*

BARBARA   David! *(*DAVID *stops, but doesn't look at her)*
Help me. *(*DAVID *looks back, not understanding. Her
voice is flat)* I know now why I asked—why I told Ted he
could come. *(*DAVID *just waits)* I wanted him to hold me.
I wanted him to make love to me. *(This is incredibly
painful to* DAVID. *He closes his eyes. Not looking at him,*

she continues) And he wanted to make love to me . . .
Oh, God, David, help me. (DAVID *just stands there*)
Doesn't it matter to you that I wanted him? Doesn't it
matter that your wife wanted him?

DAVID (*A terrible moment, then*)   No.

BARBARA   Oh, David.

DAVID (*Trying to convince himself, hard*)   It can't matter.

BARBARA (*Seeing his pain, comes to him*)   It does matter.

DAVID (*Practically keening it*)   Barbara, you are free. I am
free . . . We're all free.

BARBARA   I don't want to be free.

DAVID   I have to be . . . My life must begin!
         (*But it is bitter for him*)

BARBARA   Oh, David.

DAVID (*Anguished*)   Oh, God, Barbara, don't. I did not
come back to— I'm gone. I just came back to— I am gone.

BARBARA (*Suddenly flaring*)   All right, go! Go ahead!
You're gone. Go to your God damned freedom. (DAVID

looks at her sudden anger) But I won't come to see if you've killed yourself . . . because I'll know . . . without coming, I'll know that you have killed yourself. (DAVID, *as he looks at her, frowns*) Because you will when you have nothing but time and freedom and nobody to blame. (*She almost crouches as she goes on*) What are you going to write about? What? Tell me. You don't know anything about life. You hate life . . . this life, this ugly but only life. And you cannot write from hate, only from love, and you—you are incapable of love or loving. You can only hate and rape! Yes, it has been rape, but I wanted to be warm and open and ready . . . Do you know, do you have the faintest idea what it does to a woman not to want her husband? . . . But you have crucified us all on this dream of yours! (*She becomes almost hysterical*) You're sick . . . and I'm sorry as hell for you . . . but I hate you and I won't take the blame any more . . . and I don't give a good God damn what happens to you.

    (*She starts to cry*)

DAVID (*He is sick at heart. He waits a moment, then flatly*) You've felt this way all along, haven't you?

BARBARA (*Gasping*)   Yes . . . Yes . . . No. No! I killed a child for you. For your dream!

DAVID   What?

BARBARA   Yes, I did. For you. A child in my body.
    (DAVID *looks at her in anguish*)

BARBARA (*Spitting it at him*)   Yes.

DAVID   Not for me.

BARBARA   Yes, yes. For you. You killed the child. Your
hatred—your dream.

DAVID (*Threatening*)   Barbara, now listen.

BARBARA (*Hysterical*)   For you. I loved you. I loved you.
And it was for you . . . so that you could be free!

DAVID (*Pursuing her*)   Barbara!

BARBARA   Well, you're free now. Go ahead. Go to Nancy
. . . Go to your glorious freedom . . . I don't give a damn.

DAVID (*Still after her*)   Barbara, not for me. You did not
kill the child for me.

BARBARA (*Turning on him*)   Yes, for you . . . you and
your madness . . . you and your sickness.

DAVID   No!

BARBARA (*Hysterical, yelling it in his face*)   Yes! Yes! Yes!
Yes! Yes!
>   (DAVID *hits her. Her eyes open wide in shock and she
>   turns and runs out of the house and away*)

DAVID (*Is shocked too at what he has done, but he still yells after her, holding the hand he has hit her with aloft*) Not for me! (*He goes quickly to the door and yells again into the night*) Not for me! (*After a moment, still in shock, he says it again, but this time a pleading wail*) Not . . . for . . . me . . . (*And he sinks to the floor, trying to shrink himself in on himself. He is there for some moments, his face contorted, trying to realize yet trying to blot it out at the same time—panting, gasping. Finally his head goes all the way to the floor as he cries:*) Oh, Jesus . . . (*He remains crouching there, his breath coming in anguished gasps.*

From the shadows, very slowly TED *comes to the side of the garden. He can barely be seen. He looks across the dark garden at the figure of* DAVID *on the floor. He closes his eyes at the sight, then turns and slowly goes up to his room over the barn, and lies down on the bed, staring at the ceiling, as the lights fade out*)

Scene Two

Just before dawn, the stage is empty except for TED *lying on his bed. There is an air of great stillness, of quiet. After a few moments,* BARBARA *comes from the back shadows. She is dazed. She heads towards her door.* TED *hears her footsteps and goes to the head of the steps. He calls quietly.*

TED   Barbara? (BARBARA *stops, frowns, then turns and slowly, almost like a sleepwalker, comes to the foot of the stairs*) I have some coffee.
      (BARBARA *climbs the stairs and goes in. She sits on the edge of the bed, huddled.* TED *gives her the coffee; she shivers;* TED *puts a sweater around her shoulders. They look at each other a long time*)

BARBARA   David was here.

TED   Yes, I know. (BARBARA *looks up at him, questioningly*) When I came back—to talk to you—he was there. He left.

BARBARA   He came back to see if I had committed suicide. I yelled at him . . . I screamed at him . . . I blamed him for the child. And he hit me. (TED *sits down beside her on the bed and touches her*) I ran away, screaming . . . Didn't you hear?

112

TED   No.

BARBARA   I have been crouched up in the fields, in a place
I go to . . . trying to squeeze all life out of me . . . to be . . .
Somehow I just want to curl up, insensible, in my mother's
lap . . . Not my mother's, of course . . . but just Mother
. . . some impossibly compassionate Mother. (TED *puts his
arm around her shrunken shoulders and holds her to him,
tenderly*) I told him that I knew why I had invited you
here . . . and I was terrified at knowing . . . I wanted you
to make love to me. I'd wanted you to make love to me for
months. (TED *tightens his grip on her shoulders and bows
his head*) Only when it started happening, I couldn't. In
my dreams we were always waking up on some balcony
overlooking a peaceful lake. I wasn't shouting and screaming and drinking and clamoring to be allowed to die. I
had imagined it for months. I had escaped into that dream
for months. But suddenly you were holding me and kissing me, and it was all so different. It was hideous and I
was terrified . . . and I don't blame you for running away.

TED (*Takes his arm away from her shoulders*)   I didn't run
away for that . . . Barbara, when you were in New York,
and we had lunch at the restaurant, and I told you for the
first time about Meg's illness, about the hopelessness of
it . . . you touched my arm and looked at me. Ever since
then I have wanted you. I wanted you then—with Meg
three blocks away—dying. (BARBARA *frowns, touched
and troubled*) When Meg died, I had an almost over-
whelming desire to come to you. It was so unreal . . . I
didn't even think about your husband. I only remem-

bered your touch, the look in your eyes . . . and I wanted
you. But I thought how horrified you would be. You had
loved our marriage so. How could you understand my
wanting you right then? And as much as I needed you, I
also needed your good opinion of our marriage, and of
me. So I went away where I could be anonymous and . . .
started my senseless round of meaningless seductions on
balconies overlooking peaceful lakes . . . Any place, any
compassionate woman to get me through the night, to
help wipe out the image of Meg staring up lifelessly at
me from the hospital bed, her lips drawn back hideously.
I looked on her with love, and she stared back at me with
hate eternally frozen on her face. (BARBARA *touches his
arm*) Through all the senseless orgies, somehow I felt
the touch of your hand on my arm . . . and I said, "When
this is over, then there is peace . . . Barbara." (BARBARA
leans her head against his shoulder) When I made the
choice this morning—to go to Meg's or to come up here—
I came somehow blinding myself to the fact that you were
married. And then suddenly it was all possible, and up in
your room, there you were . . . but I stopped. This is not
what I want with Barbara. This I have had with other
women. I want Barbara forever. (*Neither of them moves.
Finally he goes on*) I came back to you to tell you all this
. . . and over there I saw David on the floor, and he was
saying, moaning over and over again, "Oh, Jesus . . . Oh,
sweet Jesus." (*He shakes his head, remembering the
sight.* BARBARA *has closed her eyes.* TED, *suddenly, ve-
hemently*) God, I never should have come here. I'm
ashamed.

BARBARA   No.

TED   I'm not a child. What did I think I was doing anyway?

BARBARA   I asked you to come.

TED   Yes, I know. But . . . (*He turns, anguished*) I wanted
so to move on. I wanted my life to move on . . . beyond
Meg. I wanted you to help me move on . . . I wanted you
to help me kill Meg.

BARBARA (*With compassion*)   Oh, Ted.

TED   But to come here, and . . .

BARBARA   Don't.

TED   I'm so ashamed . . . for everything.

BARBARA   No.

TED (*After a long moment*)   When I saw David there, I—
Eight, nine years ago, Meg and I stood at opposite ends
of a room and screamed at each other, yelled at each other
our misery, our disillusion . . . cried like children for our
lost world. But for us . . . there was no meddling visitor
out over the barn . . . and in time, thank God, we man-
aged to . . . to crawl to each other. What you saw was not
our marriage, but a kind of re-marriage out of the ashes
of our illusions . . . I take you for what you are. I will
cherish you for what you are, your complexity . . . exclud-

ing nothing this time, ugliness, meanness, hate . . . We could even say, when she knew she was going to die . . . she could even say, "I hate you because you are going on living." And I could say, "I hate you because you are dying and leaving me alone."

BARBARA   How wonderful . . . how terrible now for you— but how wonderful, really—to have loved anyone that way . . . so that the world seems so futile when they are gone.

TED *(After a long moment)*   You love David that way.

BARBARA *(She thinks about this)*   I think I loved *my* David that much . . . yes.

TED   If they find him somewhere dead in a ditch . . . (BARBARA *looks up sharply*) Even this David.

BARBARA *(Thinks about it)*   You crawled . . .

TED   If David were to die, suddenly all the love and guilt and hate would combine to make your loss . . . unendurable.

BARBARA *(After a moment)*   I don't know. *(She comes to him)* Good night.

TED   Good night.

BARBARA I don't feel anything . . . Up in the fields there, after I had yelled and screamed, I suddenly felt quite empty of all my feelings for David . . . and mysteriously, of all my desperate need for you. I feel now like some barely breathing creature waiting for some—some sensation of life. (*The telephone rings inside the house.* BARBARA *and* TED *look at each other, then* BARBARA *leaves the room and goes down the stairs, not running, but going. She stops a moment before she picks up the phone, then*) Hello . . . (*Flatly*) Hello, Mother . . . Yes, I'm all right . . . He's . . . he's gone. Mother, I don't want to talk about it on the phone . . . Mother! Mother, don't tell Roger. I want to tell him myself, in my own way . . . Yes, all right. Come back whenever you want to . . . No more now, Mother.

> (*She hangs up. In the middle of the telephone conversation,* DAVID *has come into the garden . . . At the door he has turned away as though not to go in, but finally he has turned to the door, and just stands there, looking down.* BARBARA, *as she starts for the stairs, sees* DAVID. *She pulls back and just looks*)

DAVID (*All very painful and deliberate*) I'm not drunk. (BARBARA *doesn't say anything or move*) I won't—I won't stay . . . I just . . . (*He looks up at* BARBARA, *but gets no help; he takes a step into the house.* BARBARA *turns on a light.* DAVID *winces, and she turns it off*) The baby . . . I . . . (*He stops, but then goes on*) I know you did it for me. (*With anger*) For my . . . (*He stops again; then quietly*) And I know . . . also . . . I know also that you spoke the truth about my . . . writing. (BARBARA *watches, nothing responding, and listens.* DAVID, *tired, slumps to the table, and sits*) I went back ... to my office ... and I destroyed all my notes. Everything I could find, every scrap of paper I'd ever written on.

BARBARA (*Flatly*) You shouldn't have.

DAVID (*Suddenly pleading*) God, Barbara, I didn't ask you to kill that child.

BARBARA No ... No, you didn't.

DAVID But you did it for me. I know that. (*He shakes his head in dismay and makes an animal sound of loathing*) I've known I'm no writer. I've known it for years. But I needed to be a success. I have to be somebody or I am nobody ... and this was the only way.

BARBARA (*Still flatly*) You were a writer.

DAVID I'd write two sentences, and then terrified that the rest wouldn't turn out to be the masterpiece I wanted—I needed—I'd lie on the cot up there and imagine the rest, all written, finished perfectly ... and our life all different. (*He goes on with difficulty, but with determination to say it all*) I have all the airs: the divine discontent, the longing for freedom. I don't know what to do with freedom! I have been terrified of this summer. I somehow knew that I would come to the final truth ... the final disaster ... And I always thought that if I ever accepted this truth that I would never be anything . . . I thought I would kill myself. Because I find this life intolerable without that dream . . . I still do. That is not changed. And when the papers were all destroyed, I lay down to die—in self-contempt and despair . . . But I couldn't die.

(BARBARA *just stands and listens*)

DAVID I don't understand why this dream of success is necessary to me. Other men measure out their lives in the trivia of daily tasks . . . Why for me does it have to be only days of glory? Why do I find it so impossible to live the days between?

BARBARA I don't know.

DAVID I am going to try. I am going to try to live *now* . . . I don't know how. But I am going to try. They say I am a good teacher. I will try to think of that as something to be valued.

BARBARA Yes.

DAVID (*Bewildered*) I used to find such pleasure and excitement in everything . . . as a boy. Why is it all now so flat?

BARBARA I don't know. Is it all flat for you?

DAVID Yes. I wonder if I can rediscover the wonder of the world like a child . . . They say the thumb is a miracle.

(*He stares at his lifeless open hand*) Why is it so beautiful to be a man . . . a husband . . . a father? I know it must be, but I don't know why. (*With simplicity*) I only know that I am wrong . . . and I cannot die . . . so I must learn . . . I just wanted you to know that. (BARBARA *makes a quick move to him at the table, and hugs his head to her body. His arm goes around her, and they hold each other in silence for a moment*) I am dead, Barbara . . . dead.

BARBARA   No . . . no.

DAVID   Yes.

BARBARA   No . . . Nothing that stirs such life in me is dead.

DAVID   (*He holds her tighter . . . rubs his head against her body . . .*) I may not make it.

BARBARA   I know . . . but you'll try.

DAVID   I am so ashamed . . . All the lost years.

BARBARA   Oh, my darling . . . nothing is lost. Nothing is ever really lost.
        (*They hold each other tightly. The lights fade*)

Curtain